BASICS

LANDSCAPE ARCHITECTURE

02

Nancy Rottle
Ken Yocom

ECOLOGICAL DESIGN

D0531478

Ethical: aware-
ness/
reflect-
ion/
debate

ava
academia

An AVA Book

Published by AVA Publishing SA
Rue des Fontenailles 16
Case Postale
1000 Lausanne 6
Switzerland
Tel: +41 786 005 109
Email: enquiries@avabooks.com

Distributed by Thames & Hudson (ex-North America)
181a High Holborn
London WC1V 7QX
United Kingdom
Tel: +44 20 7845 5000
Fax: +44 20 7845 5055
Email: sales@thameshudson.co.uk
www.thamesandhudson.com

Distributed in the USA & Canada by:
Ingram Publisher Services Inc.
1 Ingram Blvd.
La Vergne TN 37086
USA
Tel: +1 866 400 5351
Fax: +1 800 838 1149
Email: customer.service@ingrampublisherservices.com

English Language Support Office
AVA Publishing (UK) Ltd.
Tel: +44 1903 204 455
Email: enquiries@avabooks.com

ISBN 978-2-940411-44-3

Library of Congress Cataloging-in-Publication Data
Rottle, Nancy and Yocom, Ken.
Basics Landscape Architecture 02: Ecological Design / Nancy Rottle,
Ken Yocom p. cm.
Includes bibliographical references and index.
ISBN: 9782940411443 (pbk.:alk.paper)
eISBN: 9782940447114
1.Ecological landscape design2.Ecological landscape design--Study
and teaching
SB472.45 .R677 2011

10 9 8 7 6 5 4 3 2 1

Design: an Atelier project (www.atelier.ie)

Production by AVA Book Production Pte. Ltd., Singapore
Tel: +65 6334 8173
Fax: +65 6259 9830
Email: production@avabooks.com.sg

Name: Waterworks Garden

**Location: Renton,
Washington, USA**

Date: 1996

Designer: Lorna Jordan

Connected pools stepping
down a sculpted hillside remove
pollutants from nearby industrial
stormwater runoff before filling
a marsh that provides bird and
amphibian habitat, as well as a
recreational trail, in the midst of
an urban district.

Contents

Our built environments are often a result of intentional design decisions made to achieve a particular goal. Each decision results in impacts that alter environmental conditions locally and in sum, globally. This book examines how ecological design and planning strategies can be developed and implemented in a manner that is responsive to both human needs as well as the physical and biological processes operating in the landscape. In this regard, ecological design and planning proposes design interventions that constitute an integration of human needs and desires while supporting the health of natural systems.

Ecological design goes beyond what is 'sustainable', aiming not only to maintain status quo for future generations, but to improve upon the biological integrity of existing conditions. It aspires to generate resilience in the face of inevitable future environmental disturbances, lending a dynamic stability to both human and non-human communities. Specifically, ecological design offers opportunities to enrich biodiversity, work with natural processes, stimulate natural systems to become self-maintaining, and regenerate resources for continued use by humans and other species.

In the urban context, ecological design unites ecological theory with the allied design and planning professions' contemporary emphasis on sustainable urbanization as a solution to challenges such as global climate change, the decline of sensitive species and loss of essential resources. For example, through fostering liveable, densely developed communities, sustainable urban design makes it possible for people to live in satisfying ways that also significantly reduce the human 'ecological footprint' on the planet. Urban ecological design builds upon these practices, working with processes inherent in particular localities to enrich places and re-establish the ecological integrity of terrestrial and aquatic systems.

While urban environments may offer limited opportunities for restoring historical and biological conditions, they do provide critical opportunities for beneficial human interaction with the natural world. Research testifies to the many rewards of human contact with nature, such as physical health, mental restoration, education and inspiration. Moreover, personal connections to the natural world may foster a sense of stewardship, prompting a self-reinforcing cycle of enduring positive effects for both people and their environs.

↓
....

Name: Central Park

Location: New York City, USA

Date: 1857–1873

**Designer: Frederick Law
Olmsted and Calvert Vaux**

Central Park was conceived to
give city dwellers access to the
health-giving qualities of fresh
air, nature and activity. Today,
the 312-hectare (770-acre) park
remains the open space heart
of Manhattan, increasing the
quality of life for residents within
a dense urban environment.

Ecological design's relationship to landscape architecture

Landscape architects are uniquely positioned
to both practise and extend the field of
ecological design. The processes through
which ecology and design are entwined
are fundamental to the work of landscape
architecture. The work of many of the
profession's seminal luminaries, such as
Fredrick Law Olmsted and Jens Jensen,
is grounded in the ability to work with
environmental processes to support human
use, enjoyment and protection of the natural
world. Over the past several decades,
the study of ecological relationships has
assumed a heightened level of significance
in the allied design and planning professions.
This emergence is due in large part to an
increased awareness of the decline of local
and global environmental conditions.

Landscape architects and the ecological design process

Approaches to ecological design demand a broad understanding of the interrelationships between environmental processes and human needs. There is no such thing as a 'blank slate' when designing from a perspective that embraces ecological thinking. Physical, biological and social relationships are constantly in flux within the landscape. Ecological design seeks to identify and promote these inherent processes by relating site conditions and landscape processes to reveal and make productive these complex and dynamic relationships.

Because of the multifaceted issues of integrating ecology and design processes into contemporary social and political structures, ecological design projects are inherently interdisciplinary. Therefore, ecological projects are most successful when the expertise of scientists, planners, designers and citizens is engaged collaboratively. With expertise in design and familiarity with the natural and social sciences, landscape architects are able to integrate diverse considerations into collaborative processes and cohesive wholes, often guiding the work of ecological design teams. Further, landscape architects can bring design sensibilities to the process, often elevating mundane solutions to artful contributions that will engender human meaning, relationship and long-term care.

↑

Name: Open Space Seattle 2100 planning team

Location: Seattle, Washington, USA

Date: 2006

Designer: University of Washington Landscape Architecture

Interdisciplinary teamwork is required to address complex ecological planning and design challenges. With knowledge of the sciences and expertise in planning and design, landscape architects are well qualified to lead such teams. Here, a diverse team envisions the potential of Seattle's Open Space Network in the year 2100.

Themes and chapters

This book examines the integration of urban ecological design and planning practice into the profession of landscape architecture, and primarily focuses upon ecological design in drawing examples from the urbanized context. It is structured into two main sections. The first section (Chapters 1–3) describes the theory that supports ecological design practice by exploring the application of concepts in the ecological sciences to design. The second section of the book (Chapters 4–6) focuses more specifically on applied processes of ecological design practice and its proliferation within the field of landscape architecture. While case studies can be found in every chapter of the book, Chapters 5 and 6 heavily employ contemporary case studies to exemplify diverse applications of the practice of ecological design.

Name: Gasworks Park

Location: Seattle, Washington, USA

Date: 1975

Designer: Richard Haag

Gasworks Park was fashioned from a contaminated and abandoned coal gasification plant. Haag's design retained the dramatic defunct industrial structures and, informed by the team's soil scientist, utilized indigenous soil bacteria in humus-rich topsoil to consume the hydrocarbons and bioremediate toxins on the site's surface.

What is ecological design? –

This chapter provides an overview of the emergence and evolution of ecological design in the profession of landscape architecture. Focusing on the requirement to integrate scientific understanding with design practice, it further establishes the necessity for ecological design strategies to be integrated and applied to the design of urban environments.

Systems – Understanding how biological and physical systems are structured and function is critical to the practice of ecological design. This section of the book evaluates how systems operate across spatial and temporal scales, and how the practice of ecological design attempts to work with systems to improve human and natural conditions.

Landscape dynamics – Built environments and the processes that support them are in a dynamic state of flux, constantly adjusting to changing conditions within the environment. For landscape architects, understanding these dynamics and how built environments evolve over time is important so that designs are developed with the ability to adapt and adjust to impending change.

Project processes – This chapter presents the practical and ethical processes that are required for the implementation of successful ecological design projects, from conception to construction, to long-term stewardship. This section highlights the need for ecological design projects to be inclusive of the people they serve.

Operations – Metaphor is often used as a way to characterize and simplify complex design issues. This section suggests sets of metaphors that can be used to integrate ecological concepts into the practice of landscape design. Each metaphor is described in terms of its operational function towards achieving ecological design goals, and exemplified in form through case studies.

Places – This chapter grounds the concepts and key themes presented in the book into the places that we live and work. Implementing ecological design frameworks can be accomplished across many scales – from the residential lot to the watershed. It is important to the practice of ecological design and the field of landscape architecture to understand how a design intervention at one scale can become a catalyst for events or actions at another.

→
....
Name: Tautuku Estuary Boardwalk

Location: New Zealand

Designer: New Zealand Department of Conservation

Ecological design may enable people to become immersed in natural landscapes while also protecting ecosystems.

Ecological design is both a verb and noun. As a verb, it embodies a series of actions that include the initiation of design concepts aimed at improving environmental health, developing those concepts into plans based upon the particular qualities and processes of places, and the implementation of detailed plans while responding to the dynamics of change over time. As a noun, ecological design exists in the form of healthy, regenerative systems and components of our built environments. From parks and preserves, to buildings and streets, an ecological approach to design can be integrated into the fabric of our communities, serving as a new kind of infrastructure.

Ecological design aims to improve ecological functioning, preserve and generate resources for human use, and foster a more resilient approach to the design and management of our built environments. As an interactive approach and process, ecological design includes human as well as non-human communities and systems, applying the best available scientific theory and evidence to create resilient, sustained environmental quality.

←
....
Name: Beckoning Cistern
....
Location: Seattle, Washington, USA
....
Date: 2003
....
Designer: Buster Simpson and SvR Design
....
Inspired by Michelangelo's painting in the Sistine Chapel, the Beckoning Cistern hand reaches out to capture water from downspouts on the adjacent downtown building. The functional sculpture forms the head of a series of water-cleansing gardens that cascade down Vine Street.

What qualifies as *ecological design*? Let's start by defining these terms separately:

- *Ecology* is a branch of science concerned with the relations of organisms to one another and their physical surroundings. Ecologists have developed metrics that assess the quality or integrity of these relations within and between many types of environments.

- *Design*, as a verb, is the intentional action of planning the aesthetics and functions of objects, places or processes. As a noun, design becomes the representation of the action, often initiated as a plan or drawing.

So, we can say that ecological design is the process of actively shaping the form and operations of complex environments in such a way that composition and processes help to maintain and, if possible, increase the integrity of a region's ecological relationships.

Relationships between pattern + process

The practice of ecological design considers humans and other organisms collectively, as a distinct ecology, mutually affecting and influencing the dynamics that support environmental systems. While ecological integrity is usually characterized locally, the impacts of our collective actions often transcend immediate boundaries, requiring designers to think across spatial scales to develop ecological solutions to a problem. The generation of greenhouse gases that collectively contribute to global climate change is a prime example of this type of transboundary impact.

Applying principles of landscape ecology

From an ecological perspective, indigenous form and function differ for every locale, but landscape ecological theory does provide some guidelines for maintaining and improving upon the integrity and diversity of a region's ecological relationships. To understand and address these relationships in design, landscape architects must consider the flows of energy, nutrients and organisms, aiming to replicate or mimic the cyclical patterns inherent in natural systems, which support sustainability and regeneration over time.

← ↑
....

Name: Western Harbour and Anchor Park

Location: Malmö, Sweden

Date: 2001

Designer: City of Malmö and SLA

As part of Malmö's bid to become a carbon-neutral sustainable city, the Western Harbour district will house 600 new dwellings that produce their own energy and are well connected by bicycle and transit. Stormwater from the roofs and roadways is collected and cleaned in the waterside biotopes in Anchor Park.

Promoting resilience, biodiversity and ecological integrity

With urban environments comes the realization that no matter how effectively a place is designed, historic levels of ecological integrity may never be fully restored. A common goal, then, is to create built sites and a collective urban fabric that enables valued environmental processes and structures to be resilient to changes over time, while also promoting diversity and health in both natural and human communities.

To expand upon our definition, we advocate that ecological design aims to protect and build upon the structures and processes that enable life forms to become resilient, increase biodiversity and improve the health of both human and non-human communities.

Ecological design promotes cyclical rather than linear flows of energy and seeks to minimize waste and maximize environmental integrity from the scale of the planet to the site. At its best, it is self-renewing and regenerative. In addition, urban ecological design serves people – connecting people with nature in ways that reveal processes, promote stewardship and benefit both human and intrinsic non-human ecologies, while aiming to enhance rather than diminish local ecological integrity.

→↘
....
Name: Waitangi Park

Location: Wellington, New Zealand

Date: 2006

Designer: Wraight Athfield Landscape + Architecture Ltd

A cyclical approach to cleaning and conserving water is taken at this waterfront park. The polluted Waitangi Stream draining from a 450-hectare (1112-acre) urbanized area upstream is pumped from underground pipes through a subsurface wetland (#2) to cleanse pollutants, and then further routed through wetland channels (#3) before being collected and stored in a cistern (#5) and used to irrigate the park lawn (#10). Excess cleaned water discharges into Wellington's harbour.

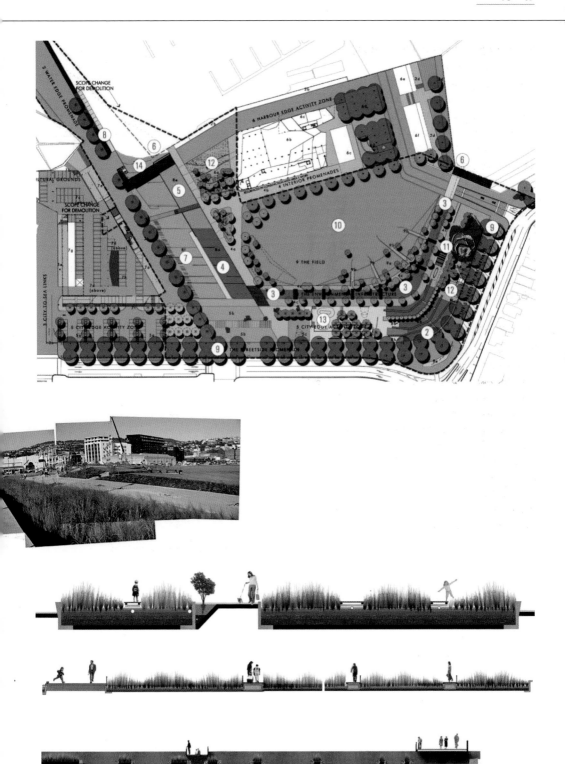

While the foundations for ecological design are continually being refined, the focus of the ecological design concepts, ideas and projects presented in this book are primarily situated within the urban context.

The urban necessity

Global populations are shifting from a predominantly rural distribution to urban. While this shift in settlement pattern represents an unprecedented transition in human history that brings many physical, social and ecological challenges, as with any frontier the cities of today are also filled with potential for improving the conditions of tomorrow. The challenges and obstacles that immediately present themselves are immense. Cities are a complex phenomenon of integrated and interwoven physical structures, and social and economic processes. They are often places of social, political and environmental inequities, where justice takes a seat behind the drivers of economy and financial incentives. Such examples are well understood in the slums of Nairobi, São Paolo and Mumbai among others; in the water quality of the Thames or Hudson Rivers, and in the high concentration of greenhouse gas emissions – the leading cause of climate change.

Taking an ecologically grounded approach to the design of existing cities and towns as well as new urbanizing areas enables communities to re-form and develop in ways that minimize environmental impacts while increasing social equality.

→
....
Name: Cheonggyecheon Stream

Location: Seoul, Republic of South Korea

Date: 2005

Designer: Seoul Municipal Government

As populations become increasingly urbanized, opportunities for people to have contact with nature become more elusive. Projects such as the Cheonggye stream restoration in downtown Seoul provide residents with opportunities to connect with restorative natural features and help to reduce the urban heat island effect.

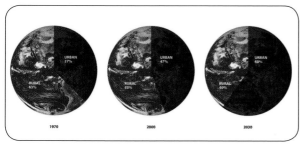

| 1970 | 2000 | 2030 |

←

Name: Rising urban populations

Designer: Tera Hatfield

Over the past several decades, the global population has transformed from living predominantly in rural settlements to urban conditions. This trend toward a more urban global community is projected to increase during the coming century.

The urban potential

Cities are products and sources of human ingenuity, cultural transformations and creativity. They reflect the vitality of our global society and epitomize social and economic progress. Cities are also part of the solution to our global environmental crisis. Urban areas that balance density with amenities can provide a high quality of life while lowering each person's ecological footprint. When citizens are able to walk, use public transit and bicycles, use neighbourhood outdoor space and access local food sources, their fossil fuel consumption and carbon dioxide emissions can be reduced.

Because many major urban centres are situated near ecologically sensitive areas such as estuaries, lakes and rivers, cities can block ecological flows and degrade environmental quality, or alternatively, they have the power to restore their land and water habitats through vision, commitment and action. With so many people now living in cities, our population centres can house rich opportunities for people to interact with the natural world, thereby supplying its restorative, educational and health benefits within urbanites' reach.

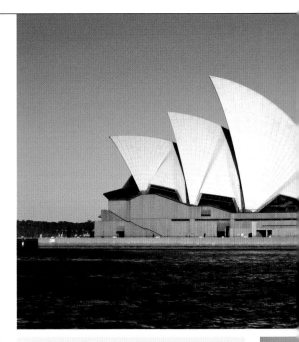

Planning for the future

Established and emerging approaches to urban ecological design are primed to address these challenges and take advantage of the opportunities they present. Fundamental change in the organization and structure of our cities requires those in the allied design and planning disciplines to reconsider their approaches for designing and managing the landscape. Focusing on the potential that cities offer, landscape architects can envision, plan and design urban environments that are diverse and healthy for not only humans, but also for the myriad of other species that share these places.

← ↑
....
Name: Sydney, Seattle and São Paolo

Location: Australia, USA and Brazil

Designer: Various

Applying ecological planning and design principles can help cities to reduce human impacts on the planet, and provide more liveable habitats for people and other species.

Sustainable development:

Development that meets the needs of the present without compromising the ability of future generations to meet their own needs.

The Brundtland Commission, *Our Common Future*, 1987

The theory and practice of ecological design has evolved in close association with societal perceptions of the relationship between humans and nature, and our theoretical understandings of ecological processes. An attitude that respects and works with natural forms and processes is at the root of the discipline and practice of landscape architecture.

Beginnings

An ecological approach to design can be traced to the early formalization of the profession by Frederick Law Olmsted in the mid-nineteenth century. Influenced by his experience of the British landscape, especially Birkenhead Park, Olmsted's projects, such as Central Park in New York, were meant to expose city dwellers to the benefits of nature. His designs for housing, roads and municipal park systems meshed with the intrinsic features of the landscape, producing 'naturalistic' designs that promoted the value of local landscape patterns.

Olmsted's design for the system of parks associated with Boston's Emerald Necklace is arguably one of the foundational projects in the field of landscape architecture. Taking an integrated approach, the project promoted urban public health and landscape rehabilitation, provided passive recreational and transportation uses in the urban core of Boston, and reduced flooding along the Muddy River. After more than a century and a half, this design remains intact – a model project for the practice of urban ecological design.

→

Name: The Emerald Necklace

Location: Boston, Massachusetts, USA

Date: 1878–1896

Designer: Frederick Law Olmsted

Olmsted's plan reshaped the Muddy River to serve as the backbone of a chain of connected parks that would solve sanitation problems, hold stormwater to reduce flooding, separate heavy traffic from pedestrian passageways, and give city dwellers contact with the natural world.

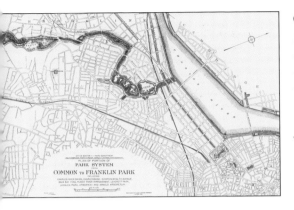

PLAN OF PORTION OF
PARK SYSTEM
COMMON TO FRANKLIN PARK

Growth of a conservation ethic

In the early and mid-twentieth century, an ethic of respect for the natural environment arose in both Europe and the US, accompanying a North American national park and natural area conservation movement. Danish-American landscape architect Jens Jensen promoted the recreation of native plant communities in his 'prairie style' approach to mid-western US landscapes, and advocated the preservation of significant landscapes and abundant parks for people to experience nature's ability to renew the human spirit.

In the Netherlands, garden designer Christiaan Broerse invented the 'heem park', following the writings of Jac P Thijsse, to create public landscapes that display aesthetic arrangements of wild indigenous plants. Biologist and early ecologist Patrick Geddes's work influenced regional and city planning, while wildlife ecologist Aldo Leopold's writings in the 1940s established a 'land ethic', arguing convincingly that human and natural communities are inextricably interconnected.

←
. . . .
Name: Jac P Thijsse Park

Location: Amstelveen, Netherlands

Date: 1942

Designer: Christiaan P Broerse

Named for a Dutch naturalist who proposed wild educational gardens in close proximity to city dwellers, the Jac P Thijsse Park displays native Dutch plant communities, especially those that are suited to peat substrates. The public garden is credited with influencing Dutch naturalistic approaches to planting design.

The birth of environmental planning

Ian McHarg's 1969 book *Design with Nature* has been heralded as a watershed event in the environmental planning movement. His book contributed to the enactment of environmental protection laws in the US and the widespread adoption of a methodology that utilized scientific environmental knowledge in urban and regional planning processes. McHarg's methodology overlays multiple systems – topographical, geological, biological and hydrological – to determine the most appropriate locations for urban, rural and wild land uses. Aimed at preserving ecologically sensitive areas, this systematic approach provided the foundation for the emergence of landscape ecology as a discipline and the development of Geographic Information Systems (GIS) – a computing program and tool that is now used ubiquitously in the allied design and planning professions.

Ecological thinking at the site and city scale

Applied to the scale of site design, environmental values and an interdisciplinary approach became manifest in numerous ways in the 1970s and 1980s, from the new habitat-based design approach for zoological parks initiated by Jones & Jones to the inclusion of wildlife habitat in park and garden designs, such as in Richard Haag's Bird Marsh in the Bloedel Reserve gardens. McHarg's own firm, WMRT, integrated natural drainage in the layout of The Woodlands housing development in Texas. Concurrently, relational concepts developed by early ecologists, such as HT and Eugene Odum, began to influence design thinking and experimentation, integrating renewable energy, aquaculture and organic agriculture into buildings and landscapes. In the UK, Allan Ruff and Robert Tregay imported Dutch ideas about ecological landscapes, promoting the infusion of nature in cities and the use of native plants and wild gardens. Anne Whiston Spirn's book *The Granite Garden* described urban environmental issues related to landscape architecture, eloquently arguing for the consideration of healthy urban nature in city design.

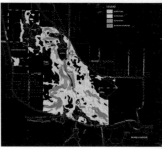

←↑
Name: Moss Garden and Bird Marsh, Bloedel Reserve

Location: Bainbridge Island, Washington, USA

Date: 1985

Designer: Richard Haag

The design of a series of four gardens at the Bloedel Reserve featured the Moss Garden anteroom, reflecting the absorbent qualities of local rainforest decay, and the Bird Marsh, which Haag designed to provide protected refuge for nesting birds.

↑
Name: McHargian Overlay Method applied to IslandWood

Location: Bainbridge Island, Washington, USA

Designer: The Berger Partnership and Mithun

The process of mapping separate layers of natural and cultural attributes and then overlaying them to determine the best locations for urban development was pioneered by Ian McHarg. In this example, the method was used to locate an educational building complex to best protect a watershed learning environment.

Sustainability and beyond

With the 1987 Brundtland Commission's definition of sustainable development, the idea of sustainable design infused mainstream design discourse. While the concept of sustainability has advanced broad acceptance of an intergenerational environmental and social ethic, the movement's core mission does not directly employ ecological concepts or propose to reverse damage or injustices already in place. Using key ecological concepts, landscape architect John T Lyle proposed the concept of 'regenerative design' for sustainable development. It advocates cyclical, closed-loop flow systems of energy and materials rather than linear, waste-generating systems of contemporary urban processes. This approach was exemplified by his design for the Center for Regenerative Studies in Pomona, California, and the integrated landscape-building systems approach at Oberlin College's Lewis Center.

This growing propensity for ecologically based design was fuelled by both academics and practitioners. In 1993, George Thompson and Fredrick Steiner edited the book *Ecological Design and Planning*. It included essays on nature and ecology, and its integration into landscape planning and design, from leading theorists in the field of landscape architecture. Sym Van der Ryn and Stuart Cowan's book, *Ecological Design*, was first published in 1996, emphasizing the role of 'place' and natural process in architectural, infrastructural and landscape design.

Restoring ecological function

During this same time in Europe, landscape designers such as Herbert Dreiseitl began integrating artful water treatment into housing projects, exemplified in the playgrounds that act as flood control terraces and the water-cleansing habitat biotopes in their master hydrological design for Ostfildern, Germany. Internationally, connected greenway corridors and networks became valued and promoted for recreation, habitat and agricultural preservation, as in Washington's Mountains to Sound Greenway.

The international landscape restoration movement grew through the Society for Ecological Restoration, advancing the application of design and management practices to the restoration of landscape structure and function. Practitioners like Andropogon applied process concepts such as the use of historic fire regimes to create and maintain native prairie landscapes, which is exemplified in their restoration plan for the Crosby Arboretum.

↑ →

Name: Crosby Arboretum

Location: Picayune, Mississippi, USA

Date: 1991

Designer: Andropogon, Edward L Blake Jr

One of the first arboreta dedicated to displaying regional native plant communities, the Crosby Arboretum employs prescribed burns to preserve its pine savanna landscapes.

Contemporary ecological thinking

In this new millennium, ecological design has taken on greater significance and with even broader considerations. Mounting evidence for human-caused climate change has stimulated global awareness and concern for impending impacts on vulnerable peoples, sensitive species and the diminishing quality of environmental conditions worldwide. As we have argued, urban ecological design helps mitigate and adapt to these changes by creating more liveable and ecologically resilient cities, softening the urban stresses that people and indigenous organisms experience while simultaneously reducing each person's ecological impact. Hence, a contemporary shift in ecological design practice is the explicit focus on urban environments, encompassing both social and environmental conditions.

Ecological urbanisms and green infrastructure

'Green urbanism', 'sustainable urbanism', 'landscape urbanism' and 'ecological urbanism' are four current movements that focus on the role of urban landscapes in contributing to the overall health of cities and metropolitan regions, and consequently to the global environment. 'Green' and 'sustainable' urbanism theories, described by Tim Beatley and Doug Farr, promote applied urban planning and design practices that simultaneously increase density while reducing environmental impacts, improving individual and community health, and increasing human contact with nature.

'Landscape urbanism' is more theoretical in its approach, offering landscape-based urban design strategies to help cities adapt to the rapid pace of urban change. Propelled by theorists such as Charles Waldheim and James Corner, landscape urbanism argues for a dynamic perspective on urban design, accounting for the complex, uncertain and multifaceted interrelationships between city and nature. 'Ecological urbanism' builds on these three theories, emphasizing the need for employing open social processes and design skill in imagining ethical, ecologically conscious futures of our inextricably linked and increasingly global cities.

↓
Name: Shanghai Houtan Park

Location: Shanghai, China

Date: 2010

Designer: Turenscape

A former industrial site located on the Huangpu River, Houtan Park now serves as ecological infrastructure, cleaning polluted river water and providing space for flood protection, food production, habitat, education and public recreation in the context of a rapidly urbanizing metropolis.

A practical application of these concepts emphasizes the ability of landscape forms and processes to function as urban infrastructure. In this regard, infrastructure is no longer limited to streets and underground pipes, but includes the benefits gained by conserving and restoring urban forests, maintaining open space, incorporating closed-loop hydrological systems and providing facilities for alternative low-impact transport. This emerging concept of integrated, high-performance landscapes reveals that designed places can provide effective ecological, as well as social and economic, services to cities and regions. Testament to the global growth of this current ecological thinking are the cosmopolitan explosion of urban bicycling networks, parks that clean water and provide habitat and systems that harvest and recycle wastewater into drinking water.

In many ways, ecological design – the act of improving upon ecological conditions through the intentional development and application of planning, design and implementation – is the work that landscape architects intend to accomplish. To do this work successfully, a landscape architect must understand the conditions, cycles and processes that form and maintain landscapes. In urban environments, this approach to design requires the effective integration of natural processes within the context of social interactions and perceptions, with desired states of ecological integrity being the goal.

Emerging theories in the ecological sciences

While the sciences produce empirical knowledge through which we understand the relationships of the world around us and beyond, this understanding is by no means static. Over the past half century, theories in the ecological sciences have begun to shift towards a more inclusive understanding of the processes and patterns that form and maintain landscape conditions. This shift in ecological understanding is based upon two primary developments. First, ecosystems once considered relatively 'closed' and independent of their surrounding context are now understood as 'open' – strongly influenced by the fluctuations and flows of biological, chemical and physical materials that pass in and out of their boundaries.

This shift in understanding means that the conceptual boundaries that once defined ecosystems have become permeable to outside influences and in return influence adjoining ecosystems. The second foundational change in ecological understanding is a shift from a perspective of equilibrium or balance between ecosystems and the populations of species they support with available resources, to a view of disequilibrium where populations and ecosystems are in a dynamic state of flux, continually adjusting to external influences and internal changes or disturbances.

When viewed together, these two changes in ecological understanding emphasize that ecosystems, whether highly urban or more natural, and the populations that they support, are dynamic and constantly adjusting to the ever-changing influences of local, regional and even global conditions. Utilizing this contemporary understanding, landscape architects are better able to comprehend the often complex interactions of landscape forms and processes that occur across time on a given project site.

↑
....
Name: SEA Streets

**Location: Seattle,
Washington, USA**

Date: 2000

**Designer: Seattle Public
Utilities**

Experimental approaches
to detaining and cleaning
stormwater on street edges
have been applied and carefully
monitored in Seattle's urban
creek basins. After finding
that the techniques were
effective in cleaning and
reducing stormwater runoff, the
landscape mechanisms have
been applied elsewhere in the
USA and abroad.

Designs that influence science

Knowledge generated in the ecological
sciences is founded upon the continued
replication of experiments that test the
response of ecological relationships. Through
this scientific method, we now know much
more about the ecological operations
of the physical, chemical and biological
environment than previous generations.
However, we also recognize that much more
knowledge is needed in order to understand
the complexities of how ecological
processes operate in specific situations.

This is where the work of landscape
architects and ecological design can build
upon our base of ecological knowledge.
Each project, in its own particular context,
becomes an applied testing ground where
both scientists and designers can more
thoroughly understand the opportunities and
constraints that ecological conditions provide.
By testing the effectiveness of their applied
design strategies, landscape architects
can build upon the current foundation of
ecological knowledge and search for new
and innovative methods for applying ideas
that will enhance ecological functioning.

Seattle Art Museum's Olympic Sculpture Park was conceived as a project that would merge art and landscape, city with waterfront, and public space with infrastructure. Formulated as an uninterrupted Z-shaped landform bridging an active railroad and arterial street, it presents four connected archetypal Northwest native landscapes across the urban hillside site: an evergreen forest valley, a dry land deciduous grove, regenerating meadows, and a tidal garden and beach. Each landscape type features sculptural works by internationally renowned artists.

The shoreline most actively targets habitat restoration, with the construction of a pocket beach, a shallow subtidal 'bench' supporting a kelp forest, and overhanging shoreline vegetation. All strategies are designed to provide food and refuge to the ecological communities that support the region's juvenile salmon populations. Scientific monitoring of this new nearshore habitat indicates rapid colonization by marine vegetation, invertebrates, and salmon, with the integrity of ecological conditions at levels similar to much older, more established beach environments in Puget Sound.

To reintroduce habitat complexity to the former brownfield industrial site, compacted surfaces have been replaced with high-humus, permeable soils; stormwater is collected, cleaned, slowed and used to create wetlands in the landscape; almost all vegetation are local native species, and ongoing grounds maintenance is pesticide free. In addition to these ecological design approaches, the park employs a suite of strategies to reduce resource use and impacts, including composting café waste and garden trimmings, water and energy conservation, and encouraging transit use and cycling. Its shoreline path provides a well-used link between the adjoining public park and Seattle's central waterfront.

Ecological approaches:
→ Preserving and enhancing shorelines and riparian corridors
→ Protecting sensitive wildlife habitat
→ Employing ecological services of wetlands, including flood control
→ Replacing exotic species with native plants of local genotype
→ Building a network of paths for walking and cycling
→ Supporting organizational capacity in local ecological restoration bodies

What is ecological design?
← Integrating science and design **Olympic Sculpture Park**

↑→↓

Name: Olympic Sculpture Park

Location: Seattle, Washington, USA

Date: 2007

Designer: Weiss/Manfredi and Charles Anderson Landscape Architecture

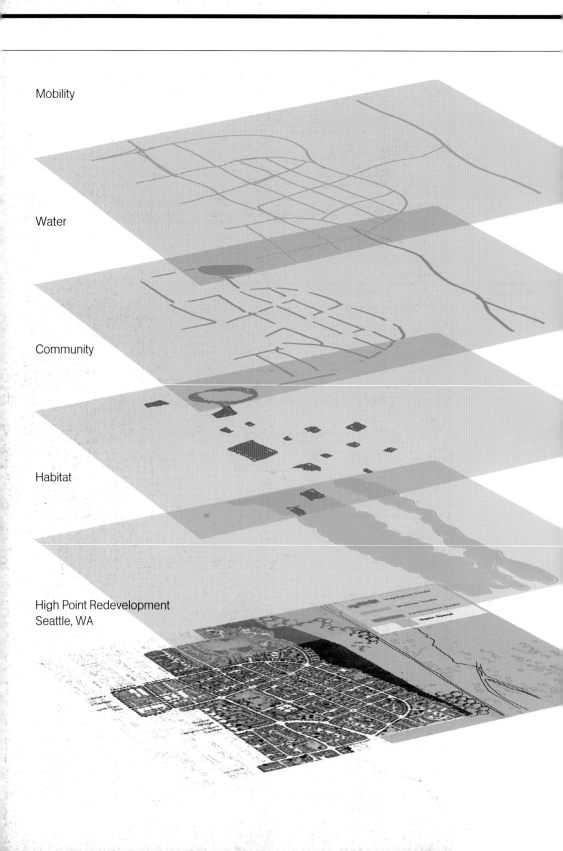

Mobility

Water

Community

Habitat

High Point Redevelopment
Seattle, WA

Landscapes are inherently complex, their structure and character defined and maintained by biophysical processes. This complexity is compounded in that these processes are spatially integrated and dynamically linked to changes over time. Any attempt to successfully address project complexity requires that the landscape architect be able to evaluate and discern not only the processes engaged within the confines of a site, but also those that influence the conditions of the site from beyond its boundaries. To understand landscape complexity, landscape architects use an intellectual framework that allows them to comprehend a site as a series of overlapping and integrated component systems.

This chapter describes a systems-based approach for understanding the conditions of a site, providing a basic understanding of the structure of both natural and built systems often found in the urban context. It further provides a platform for integrating a systems-based understanding to promote biodiversity and ecosystem health at both site and landscape scales.

←
....
**Name: High Point
neighbourhood**
....
**Location: Seattle,
Washington, USA**
....
Designer: SvR Design
....
Landscapes can be understood
as integrated systems of
spatially overlapping and
dynamic layers of physical,
biological and social processes.

We are both contained and surrounded by systems. From the basic biological building blocks of our individual bodies to the broad complexity of global climate conditions, by examining the world (or more specifically, a site) through a systems-thinking framework, landscape architects are able to comprehend the foundational processes that both form and sustain a landscape. From this base comprehension, we can further identify where and when specific design and management applications can best meet project goals and improve ecological conditions.

Structure and behaviour:

Once we see the relationship between structure and behaviour, we can begin to understand how systems work, what makes them produce poor results, and how to shift them into better behaviour patterns.

Donella Meadows, *Thinking in Systems*

Systems

Simply stated, systems represent an interconnected set of components that are organized and relate to one another to achieve some function[1]. They often exhibit behaviour that is adaptive to changing conditions, dynamic through time, self-sustaining and even evolutionary. While systems are diverse and often complex, the basic structure is relatively simple and contains three distinct parts: components, relationships and function.

1. Meadows, DH, 2008, *Thinking in Systems*. Chelsea Green Publishing Company, Vermont. 2008.

←↑
....

Name: Waitangi Park

Location: Wellington, New Zealand

Date: 2006

Designer: Megan Wraight Associates Landscape and Architecture Ltd

Waitangi Park's subsurface water filtration wetlands and cistern are related to the rest of the city's larger hydrologic system (see pages 16–17). These components provide important functions to the system, filtering and capturing water for reuse to reduce pollution to the bay and reliance upon the municipal water supply system.

Components

Components represent the key elements that form a system. They are the easiest to identify and comprehend because they are often physical, tangible elements. Components are critical to a system's operation. If one component is altered or removed, then the efficiency of the system is diminished or may cause the system as a whole to collapse. As an example, let us think of a tree as a system. The basic components of a tree consist of roots, a trunk, branches and leaves. When all components are in place the tree grows and is healthy; however, if any one of these components is removed or altered, the tree can no longer thrive and eventually dies.

Relationships

The second part of a system's structure is the set of relationships that connect components. Metaphorically, the relationships are the glue that unites the system. These relationships can take all forms, from those that are unidirectional and constant, to those that are diffuse and erratic, and everything in between. However, in general, these relationships represent the processes that enable any given system to function. Returning to our example of the tree, the relationships between roots, trunk, branches and leaves enable the tree to maintain an appropriate balance of water for survival, allowing the system to adjust and respond to changing conditions.

Function

The final aspect of a system is its function or purpose. In our example of the tree, the function of the overall system is relatively easy to understand; the flow of water between the leaves and roots allow the tree to survive despite changing moisture levels in the soil and air. However, such a clear or uniform purpose is not always so apparent. For designers and planners, the best way to understand the function of a system is to evaluate its behaviour through careful observation. Eventually, a pattern in the behaviour of the system will emerge to provide insight into its purpose. Comprehending these functions then enables the landscape architect to develop responsive and ecologically sound design solutions.

Name: The tree as a system

Date: 2010

Source: Tera Hatfield

The metaphor of a tree can be used to describe the parts of a system – components (leaves, branches, trunk and roots), relationships (structural and process oriented), and function (survival and reproduction).

While comprehending the structure and function of a particular system is necessary, it is also important for a landscape architect to understand the spatial and temporal scales at which a system operates. Scale refers to a proportional measurement upon which space and time are understood. As we have learned, ecosystems and the populations they support are dynamic, constantly in a state of flux, adjusting to changes or disturbances both internal and external to the system. To understand these dynamics when attempting to design with ecological processes in mind, a landscape architect must comprehend the scale at which these disturbances are occurring.

Scale

Scale refers to a proportion used in determining a dimensional relationship, whether in space or through time.

→
....
Name: Spatial scales

Date: 2010

Source: Tera Hatfield

The processes that form and maintain landscapes are connected across spatial scales, ranging from the planet to the site, and inversely, from the site out to the planet.

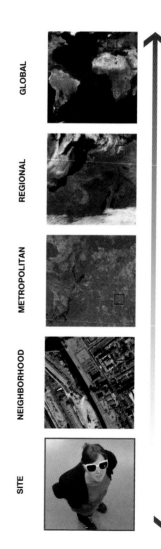

GLOBAL

REGIONAL

METROPOLITAN

NEIGHBORHOOD

SITE

Space

Spatial scale is a relative measure of the physical dimensions of an object or place. Maps are a good example for comprehending spatial scale. The relative scale of the map is dependent upon the size of the place or object being shown. If created accurately, maps can provide detailed representations of a place. The size of the place and the amount of information being represented in a map often determines the scale at which the representation is projected. For example, when examining the map of a metropolitan area or region, one centimetre might be equal to one kilometre or more, but when examining the map or plan of a site, one centimetre might represent a single metre, depending upon the size of the site.

Landscape architects must understand spatial scales in a variety of ways. First, understanding the relative proportions of spatial scale is obviously important for reading the measurements of plans and drawings, and developing accurate representations of design parameters and details. However, equally important for the landscape architect is understanding spatial scale from a perspective of landscape processes.

Changes at one scale can often disturb or affect conditions at another. For example, as the planet warms from the excess emission of greenhouse gases into the atmosphere, the polar ice sheets are melting and the oceans are warming. These changes are leading to a rise in sea levels, with the potential to impact on low-lying coastal regions around the world. While the scale of such change is immense and difficult to comprehend, a landscape architect working on a coastal site must understand the impacts of sea level rise on the place to make appropriate design decisions for long-term management.

↓
....

Name: Sea level rise on the Seattle waterfront

Location: Seattle, Washington, USA

Date: 2010

Source: Tera Hatfield and Jordan Bell

Changes to the conditions and processes that support one spatial scale can heavily affect the structure and function of landscapes at other scales. This image shows how a section of Seattle's waterfront could function with several metres of sea level rise.

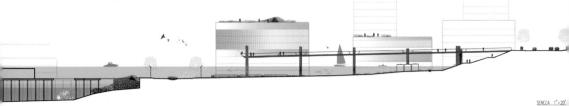

SENECA 1"=20'

Time

Understanding the influence of time on a site is also critical for landscape architects. While site designs are often represented as static and shown at a particular time, landscapes are dynamic and constantly changing. For instance, plants grow and die, and streams change course over time. In designing from an ecological perspective, landscape architects must take into account how changes to a design over time will impact, whether negatively or positively, on the ecological functioning of a site.

Temporal scales are described as either cyclical or linear. Linear projections of time are unidirectional, measured in seconds, to minutes, hours, days, years, decades, centuries and so forth. Understanding the temporal scale at which changes in process and pattern are anticipated to take place can assist a landscape architect in determining appropriate design actions. For example, the growth and establishment of a forest community is often measured in years, decades and, in some cases, centuries.

Nested within linear projections of time are periods of cyclical events. As the name suggests, cyclical events are recurring; they often determine the operations and sustenance of particular landscape and ecological processes on a site. Common examples of cyclical events include the passage of day and night, the fluctuations of tides and the annual variations in seasons.

While cyclical and linear conceptions of time can be viewed independently, they are inherently connected through the processes that form, shape and maintain landscape structure. As an example, physical changes to stream and river environments are associated with erosion – the movement of sediment through a system.

Erosion to stream banks and adjacent areas commonly occurs during high water flows that are often determined on seasonal or annual basis, and related to the amount of water in the system whether through direct precipitation, snow melt, or a combination of the two. Seasonal and annual events of flooding and erosion ultimately have long-term (linear) impacts on the structure and function of the system as a whole.

As a landscape architect becomes familiar with the types and scale of cyclical and linear events that impact on the ecological functioning of a particular site, they are better able to design for change over time.

thickening seneca stand ecologies | transistions + sea changes

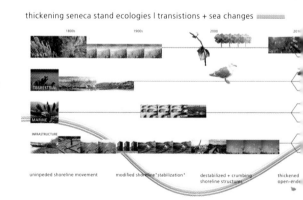

uninpeded shoreline movement   modified shoreline "stabilization"   destabilized + crumbling shoreline structures   thickened open-ende

Hierarchy

The hierarchy of systems describes the organizational structure of their operations. Levels of hierarchy in systems organization may be defined by physical or spatial characteristics, or rates of interaction, and are typically described as either 'structural' or 'control' hierarchies. Structural hierarchies refer to the spatial organization of subsystems within a larger system.

Returning to our basic example of the tree, its structural hierarchy could be described as leaves organized on branches and limbs, which are further organized along a trunk. River systems can also be described in this way as small streams are organized and drain to tributaries, which are ultimately structured spatially along the main stem of the river. This type of systems organization is typically referred to as 'nested' meaning that each subsystem is spatially contained within a larger system's organization.

In contrast, control hierarchies are not spatially explicit, but are based on the operations and function of systems. In this type of organization the presence or actions of one element in the system may exert control over the actions of another. As an example, the typical management structure of an office or business operates from a 'top-down' perspective, where the boss controls the actions and direction of work for the employees.

However, taking this example a step further, the skills, interests and capabilities of the employees may in turn affect the direction and types of work a boss or company pursues. Such control is considered 'bottom-up.' This description refers to the influence of one or a set of subsystems on another depending on the organizational rank of the system. Control hierarchies, whether in systems of office management or ecological processes, are primarily structured through the combination of 'top-down' and 'bottom-up' influences.

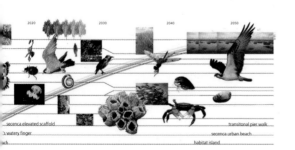

initial staging of scaffold species propogation complete
self organization habitat transitions
adaptation sequence
continued adaptation

secenca elevated scaffold
's watery finger
ach

transitonal pier walk
secenca urban beach
habitat island

←

Name: Habitat Transitions

Date: 2010

Designer: Tera Hatfield and Jordan Bell

Site conditions are constantly adjusting to accommodate changes occurring at larger landscape scales. Landscape architects must learn to work with these dynamic conditions, working across the temporal continuum.

As discussed in the previous sections, we are composed of and surrounded by systems. By viewing and understanding the world as a series of integrated and overlapping systems generally bounded in space and through time, landscape architects are able to comprehend the complexity of site conditions and landscape processes. Yet the abstract and relatively generic description of system structure that we have explored does little to identify and classify the diversity of system types that are important to the field and profession.

Open and closed systems

An initial classification of systems focuses on their contextual relationship to outside forces, materials and events. In this regard, systems are referred to as being either 'open' or 'closed'. Open systems are those that interact externally with other systems – exchanging material and energy. Closed systems are internally structured and maintained without material interaction with external environments.

Most systems are inherently open. For example, living organisms such as plants and animals are considered open because they take in external substances from the surrounding environment such as air, water and nourishment. In turn, they supply the surrounding environment with other substances. Project sites are also primarily considered 'open' – they are influenced by, and influential to, the processes and conditions of the surrounding environment.

→
Name: Road systems
Source: Shutterstock.com

The freeway and road system of an area is open, connected and utilized by motorists from both within and outside. The structure of this system as defined by freeways, arterials, connectors and residential streets often establishes the physical form and structure of a community.

Open systems | Closed systems

Open systems **refer to systems that interact externally with other systems, while** *closed systems* **describe internally structured and maintained systems involving little interaction with external environments.**

Examples of ecological and biological closed systems can be found in nearly every ecosystem on the planet. For example, in natural conditions, very little material is wasted. As plants mature, grow and die, the organic material of which they are made decomposes and the nutrients released are used to sustain future generations of plants. While there are many open systems embedded within this larger cyclical system of life, death and regeneration, the core process is closed.

Recent ecologically based design projects are attempting to mimic this type of closed systems behaviour. One example of this approach to design is the biological treatment of wastewater. Oberlin College's Adam Joseph Lewis Center, located in Oberlin, Ohio, USA, has ecologically engineered a wastewater system that combines elements of conventional wastewater technology with the purification processes of wetland ecosystems to treat and recycle the building's wastewater.

↑

Name: Adam Joseph Lewis Center

Location: Oberlin College, Ohio, USA

Date: 2000

Designer: William McDonough + Partners

Central to the Oberlin College's Environmental Studies programme, the building and site are functionally and aesthetically integrated, using recycled or sustainably harvested materials, energy efficient and passive building systems, native ecosystems, and a system for biologically treating wastewater on-site.

Natural and built systems

Another method for classifying system types is the distinction between natural and built systems. Natural systems are those systems that are structured and operate independently of human influence and intention. While the explicit operations and functions of these systems is often difficult to discern, they are primarily understood and measured by what they produce, the conditions they create, or the processes they establish. From cellular relationships to global climatic conditions, natural systems are reflective of the diversity of biological life and physical conditions on the planet. Understanding the basic constructs and operation of these systems as they interact with a site or region is critical for analysing a site's condition. The potential to improve upon these conditions is also vital to the landscape architect and ecological designer.

While there are many established methods for analysing, evaluating and understanding the conditions of a site, each, at minimum, examines the natural systems that influence a site: geology, topography, hydrology, climate and existing biology. Each system and the integrated relationships between systems form a foundation for understanding the basic physical and biological conditions of a site. For example, surface geologies and soil composition are often formed and maintained by topographic conditions and local hydrology. These conditions in turn provide the foundation for supporting biological life present on a site. The specific conditions created and supported by these natural systems form the canvas upon which design intention and action are developed, implemented and managed.

In contrast, built or human-made systems are commonly constructed and maintained with a specific end point, product, or resulting process in mind. The component parts and relationships of such a system are established to meet this purpose. Examples of built systems are as diverse as natural systems. When thinking of the physical design of urban environments, built infrastructure is the primary example used. From elaborate transportation systems combining road, train and pedestrian networks, to underground piping systems that move supplies of water into the city and wastewater out, to systems of energy generation and distribution, the built systems that support everyday life in urban and urbanizing areas are complex. Yet in understanding and analysing the conditions of a site, a landscape architect working to improve upon ecological conditions in the urban context must understand these built systems and their integrated relationships with natural systems.

↓
....

Name: Super Sustainable City

Location: Gothenburg, Sweden

Designer: Kjellgren Kaminsky Architecture

Designers are now looking toward conceptual alternatives for more efficiently integrating natural and built systems. The Super Sustainable City concept envisions Gothenburg as a city that is self-sufficient in terms of energy and food. The project seeks to drastically alter the contemporary treatment of transportation, energy, food and waste.

Integrating systems

Armed with the basic understanding of how these distinct yet related types of systems overlap, the landscape architect and planner can identify constraints and reveal opportunities for integrating the function and operation of both built and natural systems on a site. This integration forms the foundation of ecological design, which strives to creatively engage users of a site while actively improving upon existing ecological conditions. Over the past several decades, new approaches have emerged that enable this form of design integration. Landscape architects have responded with new and innovative thinking and design applications. One such approach is a perspective that planners and designers call 'green infrastructure'.

The term 'green infrastructure' is most widely used in reference to the networks of open space and natural areas that surround and penetrate cities and towns. Such references inherently recognize that these greenways provide ecological services, such as flood control, air purification, recreation and wildlife habitat. More recently, the concept has grown to describe low-impact and multifunctional infrastructure networks that support an environmentally sound approach to design and planning in urban and urbanizing areas. The recognition that green infrastructure, such as parks, urban forests and stream corridors, provide essential ecological services elevates their perceived value in a community. Further, when these elements are recognized as parts of larger systems, they can be designed and managed to achieve higher ecological and infrastructural performance.

Green infrastructure networks provide designers and landscape architects with distinct opportunities to engage design issues that span built and natural systems. Common goals addressed by green infrastructure design projects include access to public open space, improved habitat conditions for wildlife, conservation and cleaning of water resources, and reducing energy consumption and greenhouse gas emissions by offering alternative options for low-carbon transportation. While green infrastructure networks overlap in function, it is useful to identify five distinct systems, addressing open space, habitat, water, transport and metabolic energy.

→

Name: Tanner Springs Park

Location: Portland, Oregon USA

Date: 2005

Designer: Atelier Dreiseitl

One of a series of three parks that provide open-space infrastructure for a new mixed-use district of downtown Portland, Tanner Springs also collects and treats the site's stormwater and establishes a patch of meadow habitat in the city.

Green infrastructure

Green infrastructure is comprised of the natural, semi-natural and artificial networks of multifunctional, ecological and low-impact systems that provide ecological services while promoting the health of humans and their related environments.

Community open space system

The community system is comprised of the diverse public open spaces that improve liveability and connect people to one another and the places where they live. Included in this system are parks, plazas, markets, recreational spaces, civic art and the public realm of the street. Such spaces can contribute to physical, mental and community health, and make residing in dense urban contexts attractive.

The habitat system

The habitat system addresses the ecological preservation and restoration of functioning habitat to support urban wildlife and provide human contact with nature. Elements include urban forests, wetlands, streams, restored shorelines and even backyard wildlife gardens. While provision of pristine environments for rare species is limited in urban environments, the presence of varied landscape conditions can support diverse types of vegetation, insects, birds, mammals and aquatic species. Cities are often located in critical habitat areas, such as river estuaries, and are part of larger environmental systems, such as riparian corridors, and the flyways of migratory birds. Thus, the habitat system can increase local urban biodiversity while also supporting regional and global wildlife populations.

The hydrological system

Water is essential to all life and urbanization significantly affects the flow and distribution of water resources across a landscape. Sustainable hydrological approaches, sometimes called 'green stormwater infrastructure', use natural processes to treat stormwater and wastewater so as not to adversely affect aquatic habitats or groundwater sources. This approach to water management ideally harvests and cleans water for reuse, thereby reducing demands upon drinking water supply. In the form of rain gardens, wetlands, biofiltration swales, green roofs, cisterns and stormwater planters, hydrological system components may also provide habitat and enhance the condition of public open spaces.

Hydrological systems in urban environments:

→ 1) Source of clean drinking water – usually from either protected watersheds or groundwater aquifers

→ 2) Treatment of stormwater – rainwater that runs off our roofs, streets and lawns

→ 3) Treatment of wastewater – the sewage from our toilets

→ 4) Treatment of grey water – typically combined with wastewater, but this can sometimes be separated and re-used

→ 5) Source of habitat – aquatic environments require water of the appropriate quantity, temperature and chemistry to support indigenous species, as well as human health and use

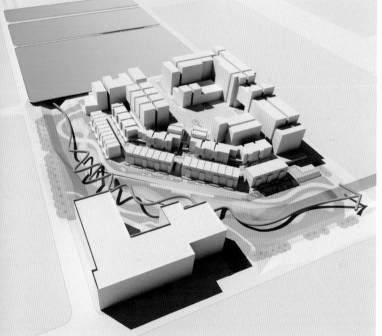

←↖
....

Name: Thornton Place

Location: Seattle, Washington, USA

Date: 2009

Designer: Mithun, SvR Design, and Gaynor Inc

Redeveloped as a 5-hectare (12-acre) mixed-use urban community, this former parking lot is designed to reveal the historical alignment of Thornton Creek and collect and treat stormwater from the surrounding streets and buildings before releasing it into the stream system.

The active transport system

Our increasing reliance upon private vehicles and the road systems they require has enormous impacts on the health of our air, water, wildlife and public realm, as well as on our individual corporeal well-being. In contrast, active transport systems provide opportunities for alternative modes of transportation, such as cycling and walking. These active modes tend to have fewer associated environmental consequences, while enhancing the physical and mental health of users, and often promoting strong social connections. Therefore, the networks that support active transport, including enhanced pedestrian environments, are considered a system of green infrastructure. Along these lines, many municipalities and communities are requiring a more complete approach to street design that provides facilities for cyclists and pedestrians within the road and associated right-of-way.

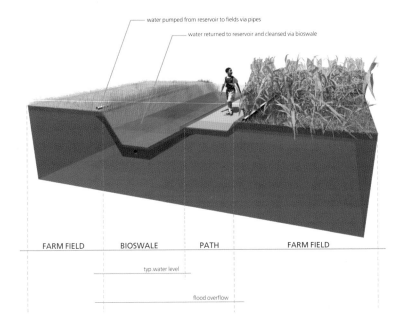

water pumped from reservoir to fields via pipes

water returned to reservoir and cleansed via bioswale

FARM FIELD · BIOSWALE · PATH · FARM FIELD

typ. water level

flood overflow

←
....
Name: Copenhagen's Bicycle Network

Location: Copenhagen, Denmark

Employing a system of raised streetside bicycle tracks, off-road trails and bridges, Copenhagen's traffic planners have prioritized cycling for both commuting and in-city travel. As a result, over half of all in-city trips, and well over a third of work and school commutes, are done by bicycle.

←↑
....
Name: Viet Village Urban Farm

Location: Tulane, Louisiana, USA

Designer: Spackman, Mossop + Michaels

This 11-hectare (28-acre) urban farm and farmers' market is designed to be sustainable culturally and environmentally. Agricultural production is organic, energy is used efficiently, water is managed on-site and waste is recycled. The market is envisioned as a place that serves the local community and aims to draw people from other neighbourhoods of New Orleans, as well as visitors from other cities.

The metabolic system

The metabolic system encompasses the processes and elements that provide energy, nourish populations, neutralize toxins and transform waste into useable nutrients. It includes clean, small-scale energy production such as wind turbines, micro-hydro, biogas digesters and local solar production. This system also includes local production and trade of food for human energy, such as community gardens and farmers' markets; composting facilities that transform organic wastes into soil amendments, and biological agents such as fungi and bacteria that digest and neutralize hazardous wastes, remediating urban brownfields for new uses. The essential work of healthy soil and its micro-organisms is sometimes separated into a sixth geologic system of green infrastructure.

The integrated nature of green infrastructure

As we have noted, a distinguishing feature of green infrastructure is its overlapping, multifunctional quality, wherein elements of one system typically provide multiple benefits, as opposed to the single functions of traditional built infrastructure. For example, rain gardens can provide flood control, water purification, aquifer recharge, habitat and community aesthetics. In contrast, stormwater pipes only convey polluted water to a downstream water body.

Although we intellectually separate systems to better understand their composition and function, both natural and built systems are interactive and integrated agents that affect the structure and dynamics of ecosystems. While the natural systems of air, water, topography and soils form the foundation of a landscape and influence the type and distribution of organisms present, built systems often impact the condition and operation of that ecosystem. Ecological design aims to promote the preservation and restoration of healthy biological systems, which support the dynamic composition of viable populations of native plant and animal species that have evolved over many millennia.

Biodiversity defined

The term biodiversity refers to the complete variety of life on earth, an important aspect and indicator of healthy biological ecosystems. The term is inclusive of all scales: from ecosystem diversity (the variety of ecosystem types and associated biological communities); to species richness (the number of species in a given area); to genetic diversity (the variability in the genetic make-up among individuals of the same species). In addition, the structures, processes and interactions operative in a biological community are considered key aspects of biodiversity. Research on the world's ecosystems has shown that global biodiversity is declining at an alarming rate, making issues of biodiversity of paramount importance in conservation planning and ecological design.

←↑
....

**Name: View across Roto
Kawau at ZEALANDIA**

**Location: Wellington, New
Zealand**

Date: 1995–

Comprised of artificial lakes
surrounded by regenerating
forest, this urban sanctuary
is the final refuge for many of
New Zealand's rarest wildlife
species. The 225-hectare (556-
acre) sanctuary is managed to
promote and maintain native
biodiversity. A special fence
prevents predation by exotic
predator mammals and has
been an effective strategy
in establishing safe habitat
for New Zealand's sensitive
ground-dwelling birds.

Why does biodiversity matter?

Maintaining the richness of species and
ecosystems on earth is important for
several reasons. First, biological systems
and organisms provide essential services
for humankind. From the smallest micro-
organisms that form the basis of ocean
food chains, to carbon-absorbing tropical
and boreal forests, these dynamic physical
and biological interactions of the world's
ecosystems support human survival
and maintain an atmosphere that allows
for the existence of life on the planet.
Unknown species may hold promise as
remedies for disease, hunger and other
future challenges. Our discovery and
management of these resources will
depend upon the science of, and education
about, diversity of species and systems.

The variety of life that has developed
over hundreds of millions of years si the
foundation for a deep aesthetic appreciation
of life on earth. Many argue that we have a
responsibility to leave an ecologically intact
world to future generations, not only for the
pragmatic services that it will provide, but
also for the sense of wonder it provokes. In
addition, many feel that we have a moral
obligation to protect the natural world for its
intrinsic value, for the benefit of all species.

Biodiversity and resilience

In addition to these compelling imperatives, biodiversity is important because it increases the resilience of an ecosystem to respond and adapt to change while maintaining its core function and character. Moreover, biodiversity provides for a redundancy of functions spread across multiple species, to cope with pressures that might eliminate, or severely limit, the population of one species that others depend upon. For example, consider the impact of losing a pollinator species essential to seed and fruit production in an ecosystem. Over time, the decrease in reproductive capacity of the species that relied on the pollinator would likely have dramatic effects on the condition and structure of the ecosystem as a whole.

A well-established level of biodiversity in an ecosystem allows species to fill the gap left by the loss of one pollinator. Considerations for biodiversity planning are increasing on a global scale as the projected disturbances of climate change – such as hotter temperatures, more rain and drought, and heavier storms with consequential flooding – will likely have detrimental long-term impacts on human settlements as well as the biological composition of ecosystems across the world.

↑→
. . . .
Name: The High Line

Location: New York, New York, USA

Date: 2009

Designer: James Corner Field Operations and Diller Scofidio + Renfro

This 2.33 kilometre (1.45-mile) New York City park is built on a section of the former elevated freight railroad spur called the West Side Line, which runs along the lower west side of Manhattan. The design for the park reuses and reactivates the existing infrastructure, repurposing the line as public open space and inserting additional pathways for people, plants and insects.

The greater the biodiversity, the greater the ability to adapt to change. Reduced biodiversity leaves an ecosystem unhealthy and vulnerable.

Schaefer et al 2004

Systems

← Green infrastructure systems **Ecosystem health and diversity**
Waitakere and Twin Streams →

Biodiversity and ecosystem health in the urban context

Why promote biodiversity in urban areas? In most cities, there are relatively few opportunities to promote biodiversity and preserve the existence of ecologically sensitive species. However, maintaining biodiversity in urban environments provides numerous benefits.

First is the impact on human health and well-being. For most of its existence and evolution, the human species has depended upon and lived in close proximity to the natural world. Biologist EO Wilson theorizes that humans have a predisposed affinity for nature, which he terms *biophilia*. Scientific studies overwhelmingly document the benefits of contact with nature, including recovery from illness, mental health, relaxation, concentration, lowered crime rates and higher learning performance. If populations are to experience these benefits, as well as a sense of appreciation and wonder for life on earth, then they require first-hand contact with the inspiring diversity of organisms and biological communities in their home territories.

In addition, cities and metropolitan areas are nested within larger ecosystems and the processes and species they support. Therefore, urban areas often play an important role in determining the health and biodiversity of broader ecological systems.

Consider the hazards that migrating butterflies, birds and fish must face to move between their birthplaces to seasonal feeding grounds, often travelling across continents and hemispheres. For example, salmon must swim through polluted lakes and bays of coastal cities, with hardened shorelines devoid of shelter, to get from their hatching and rearing grounds in streams and lakes to the oceans where they spend most of their lives. Cities can provide hospitable stepping stones for many species, while both human city dwellers and local ecosystems benefit from the age-old interactions with these seasonal visitors.

Name: Tianjin Qiaoyuan Wetland Park

Location: Tianjin City, China

Date: 2008

Designer: Turenscape

This award-winning park integrates a diverse collection of habitat conditions for native species while serving to improve water quality and provide open space access for surrounding residents.

How to enhance landscapes for wildlife and biodiversity

1. Provide maximum vegetative cover
2. Use native vegetation
3. Provide escape cover vegetation for small animals
4. Provide structural diversity in vegetation layers

adapted from Livingston et al, 2003

CASE STUDY

For the last two decades, Waitakere, New Zealand, has built itself upon values of preserving and enhancing its Green Network. Encompassing the city's system of connected mountains, coastlines, stream corridors and urban areas, the programme values the functions and processes of its diverse biological network and the ecological, economic and social services that it provides.

Waitakere's Twin Streams project exemplifies the city's natural systems approach and its goal of enhancing community resilience. Responding to local flooding problems and pollution in Waitamata Harbour, the programme has converted urbanized lands along 54 kilometres (34 miles) of two stream corridors within the city to provide flood storage and improve habitat conditions and functions. The focus and process of stream restoration is aimed at bringing awareness to integrated catchment-wide issues of water conservation and aquatic quality, and to act as a springboard to promote more sustainable household practices throughout the city.

The Twin Streams project is also aimed at building social capacity by employing community organizations and engaging volunteers and school groups in the ecological restoration process. As part of this programme, residents have installed over half a million plants, primarily sourced from local genetic stock, with an estimated capacity to absorb the carbon dioxide emitted from 21,000 vehicles travelling 15,000 kilometres (940 miles) per annum. In addition, over 9 kilometres (6 miles) of cycle paths and walkways give public access to the restored Twin Stream sections, and an integrated arts programme engages diverse local communities in creating expressive cultural markers along the stream corridors.

Ecological approaches:

→ Preserving and enhancing shorelines and riparian corridors

→ Protecting sensitive wildlife habitat, including large patches

→ Employing ecological services of wetlands, including flood control

→ Replacing exotic species with native plants of local genotype

→ Building a network of walking and bicycle paths

→ Supporting organizational capacity in local ecological restoration bodies

Systems

← Ecosystem health and diversity **Waitakere and Twin Streams**

←↙↓
....

Name: Waitakere Green Network and Twin Streams

Location: Waitakere, New Zealand

Date: 2003–2012

Designer: City of Waitakere

Noted ecologist Richard Forman describes the term landscape as 'what one sees out the window of an aeroplane'. He refers to a broad and sweeping view that encompasses one's surroundings, and can be described in physical terms by its form and pattern. However, as previously noted, landscapes are dynamic and shaped by systems of ongoing physical, biological and social processes. These processes create patterns on the landscape that link the scales of space and time. The material, shape and structure of these patterns form what is commonly termed the land mosaic – a complex fitting together of the heterogeneous patterns and processes that form and sustain a landscape.

The study of these land mosaics and their formative landscape processes is the field of landscape ecology. Landscape architects and planners utilize the principles developed through the science of landscape ecology to plan and design landscapes in order to improve the ecological health and diversity of a particular place. This chapter examines the basic principles and processes of landscape ecology and current theories of landscape dynamics. It discusses how these concepts can be applied in design and planning to engender dynamic landscapes that are resilient, sustainable and regenerative.

←
....
Name: Aerial view of a landscape
....
Location: Boise, Idaho, USA
....
The term landscape generally refers to a large area shaped by integrated systems of physical, biological and social processes.

Much like the elements of a system, a landscape is comprised of components (form), relationships and functions. The *form* of the landscape refers to the spatial arrangement of physical materials. From mountains to rivers, from boulders to trees, from farmhouses to high-rises – these components and their distribution across the landscape create its pattern. The *functions* of landscape refer to the flow of materials and energy through the patterns of landscape structure. These flows represent process and relate to the impacts associated with the movement of water, wind, plants, wildlife, people. They also relate to metabolic processes across time and scales, from biological communities at the site scale, to the process of plant community succession at another.

The form and function of landscapes are dynamic, continuously evolving and adapting to changing conditions over time.

← ↑
....
Name: IJburg

Location: Amsterdam, The Netherlands

Designer: Palmbout Urban Landscapes

In this project, the designers created a new urban lobe into the bay by integrating an archipelago of neighbourhood development, parks and wetlands. This enabled the continued functionality of ecological processes, instead of using traditional modes of diking to form new land.

Landscape dynamics

The form and function of landscapes Dynamic equilibrium and resilience →

Matrix

The matrix is the dominant land use or habitat type in a landscape. The matrix on any given landscape can range from high-density urban development as found in the major cities of the world to the tropical rainforests of the Amazon basin, and all conceivable conditions between. Typically, the dominant land use type is defined by its spatial area. However, the processes and conditions that support a particular land use may have a substantial influence on the conditions of the landscape. For example, the development from an urbanizing landscape may only comprise a small portion of the overall mosaic of the land, but the infrastructure and location of the development may have significant impacts on the processes and conditions of the landscape as a whole.

For a landscape architect planning and designing with ecological implications in mind, it is important to comprehend the overall mosaic and dominant land use of a site and its surrounding context. Based on the goals and objectives of a particular project, it is critical to work with existing conditions and identify opportunities that enhance ecological function and health.

Corridors

Corridors are linear elements of the landscape that often function as conduits between patches. They can range in type, size and quality from a hedgerow between houses to a stream and riparian corridor that facilitates the movement of not only animals and plants, but also people, water and nutrients. While the existence of corridors promotes movement of species and material across a landscape, they can also have negative impacts on a population. Depending upon the size and condition of corridors and the habitat requirements of species that use them, corridors can filter desired species while enabling transference of less desirable invasive species.

Points of intersection in corridors can also serve as barriers, reducing the ability of species to move between patches of habitat. For example, a road built across a riparian and stream corridor can effectively block the movement of fish and amphibians in a system. While ecological corridors do have negative consequences, it is generally assumed that the provision of ecological corridors in urban areas creates opportunities for re-establishing a larger, connected network of positive open space conditions.

For the landscape architect, it is important to work with local ecologists to determine the most appropriate location of design elements and to provide suitable corridors that facilitate the movement of desirable species across a landscape.

Edges and boundaries

All patches and corridors contain edges that form the transition from one habitat to the next. Edges may be distinct, such as the boundary between a cultivated field and surrounding forest, or less so as two habitat types merge and overlap based on natural biotic and abiotic conditions in the landscape. The term 'edge effect' is used to refer to the different processes that occur along the edges of a patch or corridor in comparison to its interior area.

For most of the past century, wildlife management planning and practices have promoted increasing the overall quantity of habitat patch edges. This arrangement was considered beneficial to wildlife conditions as it increased overall biodiversity in an area as species that prefer adjacent habitat types become interspersed within and along these edge conditions. However, recent research has shown that increasing the amount of edge in a particular patch or corridor often reduces the overall area of interior habitat conditions, thereby reducing the quality of these areas for many species that are intolerant of edge conditions and human disturbances.

Depending upon the location and surrounding context of a particular site, a landscape architect must evaluate the potential impacts and benefits that the edge effect may have on the species that utilize the area.

↑→

Name: Trillium Projects (Genesee Meadow and Pritchard Beach Wetland Park)

Location: Seattle, Washington, USA

Date: 1996

Designer: Charles Anderson Landscape Architecture

Edges represent areas of transition within a landscape. Typically areas of increased biodiversity, they can also limit the area accessible to species that require large tracts of core habitat to proliferate.

Patches

Fragmentation is a process in which the matrix of a landscape is disturbed by natural changes or human actions, isolating areas of the matrix into patches. Landscape patches are fragments of distinct landscape form within a matrix of relatively homogeneous landscape conditions. They are distinct from their immediate surroundings by the composition of their structure. While the basic definition of the term creates consistency in determining what a patch is, the composition, size, number and location of similar patches in a particular landscape often determine the viability of plant and animal populations that use these habitat types.

Name: Patch

Location: City of Rocks National Reserve, Idaho, USA

Patches represent a landscape or habitat type that is distinct from surrounding conditions. Depending on the scale at which the landscape is observed, patches can be as small as a single tree in a sagebrush prairie, or as large as a forested slope on the side of a mountain.

Patches of heterogeneous landscape types are created in several ways. In undisturbed, natural landscapes, patches emerge through the variability of environmental conditions such as soil types, water availability, or microclimate conditions, as well as by processes of disturbance such as fires, flooding, or major storm events. People also create patches across the landscape through changing land uses as seen in logging, agriculture and urban development. In these cases, the dominant conditions of a landscape often become increasingly fragmented with additional development and intensity of use.

Depending upon the scale of the site or landscape being considered, the size of a patch can range from a single tree to an entire forest preserve. From an ecological perspective, patches are commonly considered to be islands of a particular or preferred habitat or land use type surrounded by an area of less favourable habitat. Patch size and relative location to other similar patches are important. In general, the size of patches matter – the larger the patch, the greater the potential for higher levels of biodiversity. Further, the density of patches within a given landscape determines the ability of species to travel between these areas. The closer habitat patches are to one another, the greater the likelihood that species will be able to move between these areas.

Over the last several decades, ecologists have shifted from an equilibrium – or balance of nature – understanding of ecosystem dynamics, to a perspective that recognizes the role of disturbance and the external and internal flow of material and energy through a system. Rather than viewing ecosystems as closed and operationally autonomous, it is now understood that ecosystems are strongly influenced by the contextual inputs or flows of material and energy from outside of the system, such as water, nutrients, airborne seeds and pollen, and people. These flows impact ecosystems through time with sometimes lasting effects.

Dynamic equilibrium

This emerging understanding of ecosystem dynamics is a shift from a static perspective of equilibrium and balance to a view of ecosystems that are in a constant state of flux, dynamically accommodating change, emerging processes and evolving forms.

Natural disturbances (such as fires or a tree falling in a forest) and human actions (such as urban development) are thought to arrest the succession of portions or patches of the landscape. These disturbances can potentially foster diverse compositions of species and processes within larger ecosystems.

Ecological research is finding that an intermediate level of disturbance in any given landscape is optimal for establishing high biodiversity: not too much or too often for the landscape to recover, but enough to support a diverse age structure of existing species while creating conditions for other species to establish. At the same time, while older, less dynamic ecosystems, such as old-growth forests, may provide habitat for fewer numbers of species, they may support particular species that require more stable conditions, contributing to overall ecosystem and species diversity.

Landscape dynamics

← The form and function of landscapes **Dynamic equilibrium and resilience**
Resilient + sustainable + regenerative design →

→
....

Name: Crosby Arboretum

Location: Picayune, Mississippi, USA

Owner: Mississippi State University

The managed and prescribed burning of some landscape types assist in supporting and maintaining the diversity of native biota in these habitats by controlling undergrowth and supplementing the soil with nutrient rich ash.

←
....

Name: Old growth forest

Location: Mount Rainier National Park, Washington, USA

Forests are in constant states of flux as trees grow, shade levels and soils change, and flows of nutrients and organisms shift. Until cataclysmic events cause forest structure alteration, old growth forests provide longer periods of stability for sensitive organisms.

Resilience and cities

Resilience theory views systems as complex, self-organizing, unpredictable and responsive to spatial and temporal changes. In relation to ecosystem processes, resilience is closely associated with the concept of dynamic equilibrium. For example, while ecosystems may reach a phase of relative stability, an extended disturbance or series of disturbances – such as storms, species invasion, excessive nutrient loading, or land conversion – may force the ecosystem to a threshold where ecosystem processes can no longer be supported. Such thresholds or 'tipping points' may be avoided in systems that are resilient. For example, abundant biodiversity, as was discussed in Chapter 2, lends resiliency to ecosystems through varied species performing similar functions.

The concept of resilience is now being applied to the planning and design of cities, which, like natural ecosystems, are complex and adaptive to the myriad flows constantly moving within and through them. These flows include natural elements, such as solar radiation and weather, and human elements such as transport, trade and resource use. Like ecosystems, resilient cities also benefit from redundancy in systems; when systems overlap, the functions of an overloaded or failed system may be replaced by an alternative system. The overlapping ecological services of urban forests are an example of green infrastructure that contributes to resilience in urban systems, in decreasing stormwater flows, helping to maintain stable urban temperatures, and providing habitat for urban wildlife.

Landscape dynamics

← The form and function of landscapes **Dynamic equilibrium and resilience**
Resilient + sustainable + regenerative design →

↑
....
Name: Temporary pedestrian street

Location: Quebec City, Canada

Date: 2010

This shopping street is closed to vehicles for parts of the day, enabling the roadway to support overlapping modes of movement.

↑
....
Name: Pedestrianized Broadway Avenue at Times Square

Location: Manhattan, New York, USA

Date: 2009

Designer: Gehl Architects and New York City Transportation

Resilient cities are seen as complex and able to adapt to changes in flows over time. Overlapping and redundant systems, such as active transport systems (walking and cycling) and the ecological services provided by urban forests, may increase a city's resilience to catastrophic changes.

Applying dynamic equilibrium theory to design

Bearing in mind these approaches to understanding ecosystem dynamics, primary goals of ecological design are often to create landscapes that are adaptive yet resilient to disturbances, self-regulating in their processes, and self-renewing in form and composition. Such landscapes may provide the benefits of ecological services to reduce stresses on scarce resources. Through design, landscape architects can utilize anticipated site flows to catalyse and maintain processes that may self-generate and improve ecological health, recognizing that the conditions of the landscape will change over time.

The landscape architect typically works with professionals in other disciplines, such as hydrologists, ecologists, wetland specialists and engineers, to understand processes, quantitatively predict changes in a system, and establish general target conditions over time. It is important for landscape architects to understand the basic operations of these processes in order to work creatively with others involved in the design process, and to communicate effectively with other team members. In addition to working at the site scale, it is critical to maintain awareness of the interactions of flows and processes at adjacent ecosystem scales, both to understand external influences upon the site, as well as the role that the site may play in improving ecological conditions of both larger and smaller systems that may interact with the site.

Landscape dynamics
← The form and function of landscapes **Dynamic equilibrium and resilience**
Resilient + sustainable + regenerative design →

↑

Name: Amager Strandpark

Location: Copenhagen, Denmark

Date: 2005

Designer: Hasløv & Kjærsgaard Arkitektfirma

This extensive public beach project developed a new island that provides popular deep-water swimming and boating access, as well as long stretches of native dune habitat. The design of the 2-kilometre (1-mile) long island works with the tidal energy of Øresund Sound, enabling the beach sands to be replenished over time by the cycles of the tides.

The terms 'sustainable', 'regenerative', and 'resilient' are often used interchangeably with ecological design. This section describes each term individually, and explores the commonalities and distinctions in their application.

Design for resiliency

A resilient design anticipates future disturbance such as flood, fire, wind, storms, sea level rise, climate change, and alteration in human use, and establishes capacity for the designed place to adapt to changes while maintaining its core ecological functions.

Resilient designs recognize hierarchies of scale in systems. Planning and design interventions are aimed at increasing the quality of conditions in the overall ecological system, and at supporting the services that they provide towards avoiding infrastructural system overloads and impacts from catastrophic events. An example of ecological services contributing to a system's resiliency is evident in the role that coastal estuary and mangrove forests play in protecting cities from coastal flooding.

Another form of integrating resiliency planning into urban environments is the establishment of multiple forms of transportation systems: automobiles, public transport, cycling and walking. While redundant, the systems allow for flexibility and freedom of movement, and enable one or more systems to accommodate users if another is hindered.

→
....
Name: Center for Urban Waters

Location: Tacoma, Washington, USA

Date: 2010

Designer: Perkins and Will Architects; Swift & Co Landscape Architects

This building features systems that reduce reliance upon regional resources. The structure's solar orientation, green roof and use of ground source heat significantly reduce energy requirements, while lab water is recycled for toilet flushing and irrigation.

←

Name: Bicycle parking ramp

Location: Amsterdam, The Netherlands

Date: 2001

This bicycle parking garage located outside Amsterdam's Central Station holds over 7000 bicycles.

Sustainable design

The primary goal of sustainability is to conserve resources, managing them for use, but with little to no net loss over time. This focus on resources implies that they are for human use and consumption, and include materials, such as petroleum, wood and metals, as well as ecosystems and the ecological services that they provide. The efficient use of materials and energy, including methods of recycling and reuse, is emphasized.

With sustainable design, contemporary conditions are typically conserved rather than improved upon. Sustainable design addresses a set of tripartite goals, which are to conserve not only environmental resources, but also social and economic values. From a sustainability perspective, projects that address all three of these goals provide maximum benefit to society.

Regenerative design

Regenerative design goes further than sustainable and resilient design, focusing on restoring ecosystem health and generating new resources for human use. A regenerative perspective aims at catalysing natural and human processes to improve environmental conditions over time, and to spiral resource production and ecosystem integrity upwards rather than downwards. Closed loop rather than linear systems are typically used to conserve and regenerate resources and ecosystems: an example is water harvest treatment in wetlands that also provides habitat, and then reuse of that cleansed water in dwellings or industry. Especially applied to products, this perspective is sometimes referred to as 'cradle-to-cradle', where products are continually re-purposed to make new materials, and waste is considered valuable material for reuse.

→
....
Name: Trajectory towards regenerative design

Designer: The Integrative Design Collaborative

This diagram illustrates levels of contributions that design can make – from degenerating, to neutral, to regenerating.

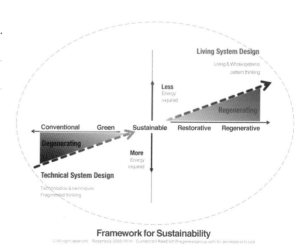

Framework for Sustainability

The regenerative approach considers both societal needs and the long-term integrity of natural systems. This is especially noticeable in cities where human interaction and attachment are seen as critical for effective regenerative design; human actions are usually required to assist with the regeneration of landscapes that are subject to so many urban-generated flows. Therefore, the role of public engagement with the site and design process is important, as are artful elements and approaches that foster long-term protection and stewardship.

Ideally, a landscape architect will incorporate all three of the previously discussed design perspectives: resilient, sustainable and regenerative. In this way, landscapes will be created to be adaptable to changing conditions while maintaining fundamental integrity and providing overall system resiliency. They will conserve resources in their materials and construction processes while also addressing social and economic values. Finally, they will regenerate material resources and provide improved ecological and human conditions that are self-regulating, self-renewing and supportive of diverse ecologies.

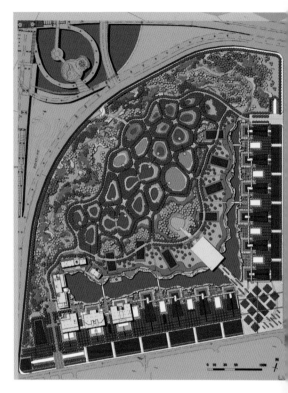

↑

Name: Tianjin Qiaoyuan Wetland Park

Location: Tianjin City, China

Date: 2008

Designer: Turenscape and Peking University Graduate School of Landscape Architecture

Regenerative design improves upon environmental conditions, increasing ecological integrity and resource production. This project transforms a historic garbage dump into a vibrant urban park, increasing accessible open space for residents while improving water quality conditions and reintroducing native vegetation to the area.

CASE STUDY

Major world cities such as Toronto are in transition, needing to re-integrate strategically important post-industrial landscapes while reframing their interactions with the natural environment. The Port Lands Estuary proposal is unique among these efforts by virtue of its size, scope and complexity. In this proposal, the engine of transformative urbanism is a radical repositioning of natural systems and attendant landscapes, transportation networks and urban environments. The imperative of sustainable flood control leads to relocating the river mouth, and a renewed recognition of the functional and experiential benefits of river ecology makes it the symbolic and literal centre around which new neighbourhoods can be constructed.

This master plan unites innovative design approaches from landscape architecture and urban design with innovative scientific approaches to natural reclamation at the scale of the city and the region. Within this plan to recycle 113 hectares (280 acres) of Toronto's waterfront, the Port Lands Estuary proposal fuses the client's major programmatic initiatives into a single framework that will simultaneously make the site more natural (with the potential for new site ecologies based on the size and complexity of the river mouth landscape) and more urban (with the development of a green mixed-use district and its integration into an evolving network of infrastructure and re-connection). Both the urban and the natural elements of the landscape introduce complex new systems to the site that will evolve over the course of many years, creating interim conditions, each interesting in its own right, which give form, focus and character to the development of the neighbourhood.

Ecological approaches:
→ System-based approach to urban design
→ Introduces a phased approach to design
→ River and estuary restoration
→ Creation of aquatic and terrestrial habitat
→ Increase in accessible open space

↑ ↗ →

Name: Port Lands Estuary

Location: Toronto, Ontario, Canada

Date: 2007

Designer: Michael Van Valkenburgh Associates, Inc in collaboration with AECOM, Applied Ecological Services, Arup, Carpenter Norris Consulting, GHK International Consulting, Greenberg Consultants, Limno Tech, MMM Group Ltd, Mack Scogan Merrill Elam Architects, RFR Engineering, Transsolar Energietechnik GmbH

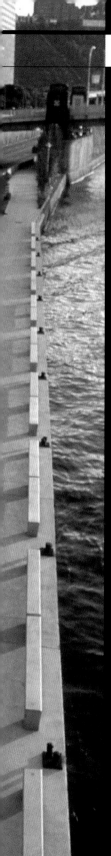

The themes presented in this book – systems, scale, dynamics and diversity – all reflect the complex conditions that a landscape architect must consider when taking an ecological approach to project design. To successfully implement these themes, the landscape architect must guide a project through numerous phases, from site and context analysis through to design, detailed development, construction and long-term stewardship.

Ecological design incorporates the understanding of ecological conditions and processes throughout these project phases; a project's success is dependent on responsive and thorough design, conscientious construction practices and quality, and the site's ability to sustain desired conditions and processes over the long term. Therefore, a significant aspect of achieving and maintaining ecological integrity is developing and implementing resilient physical and social structures that support a project long after it is constructed.

This chapter outlines both ethical and practical approaches to the design, construction and long-term stewardship of projects so that they may serve to protect, rehabilitate and potentially regenerate ecosystem health.

←
....
Name: Allegheny
Riverfront Park
....
Location: Pittsburgh,
Pennsylvania, USA
....
Date: 1994–1998
....
Designer: Michael Van
Valkenburgh Associates,
Inc
....
Landscape architects guide projects through planning, design, the production of construction documents and consultation during the construction process. Awareness of practices that will increase ecological performance is necessary at each of these stages.

The planning, design and realization of an ecological project is usually a complex and lengthy process involving many players, and often relying upon leadership from the landscape architect. Key to setting a project on an ecological trajectory is gaining an understanding of the conditions of the site, the systems in which it interacts, and the site's potential to positively affect and utilize flows through and within it. Knowledge of the environmental qualities, threats and levels of biological integrity on a site will help the landscape architect to set target conditions for the design: what defines ecological integrity on the site, and what processes need to be maintained, catalysed, or inhibited? What are essential conditions and appropriate goals for the project? What should be protected? What is possible to restore, rehabilitate, or regenerate? What ecological function or performance can be stimulated within an entirely new landscape? What landscape structures can be established that will support desired ecological processes?

Primum non nocere: First do no harm

Establishing a high degree of ecological integrity through intentional design activities is a challenging endeavour; many studies have documented the failure of environmental projects to achieve their ecological goals. Therefore, the first maxim of ecological design is to protect the existing integrity of functioning biological systems wherever possible. The operational action of the designer might consist of identifying areas of ecological integrity and working to preserve those conditions. Along these lines, landscape architects should site buildings and infrastructure that possess lower ecological function appropriately. An overlay approach to site design utilizes a technique that layers site conditions and functions to identify the most suitable land for development. Common options in site design are clustering buildings and roads to reduce the overall construction footprint, while locating development close to existing facilities and public transit, thus minimizing the potential of larger-scale impacts related to transportation emissions of a project over the long term.

→
....

Name: IslandWood

Location: Bainbridge Island, Washington, USA

Date: 2002

Designer: Mithun and The Berger Partnership

The Pacific chorus frog spends a part of its life cycle in wetlands and another part in the moist Pacific Northwest forest, such as those found at IslandWood.

←

Name: IslandWood

Location: Bainbridge Island, Washington, USA

Date: 2002

Designer: Mithun and The Berger Partnership

In planning where to place the cluster of educational buildings on the wooded campus site, designers first mapped the landscape systems using the McHargian overlay process. The layers were then combined to see which parts of the site needed to be preserved and where the buildings would have the least impact on the ecological integrity of the watershed.

Restoration and rehabilitation

Most landscapes and sites have already been impacted by human actions. When working on a degraded site that has adequate potential, design teams should strive to restore and rehabilitate the site's native ecological functions, especially so when the conditions of the site, such as soil health and water flows, are consistent with historic functions. If the site has been radically changed, then the designer must identify the requirements of successful restoration and determine if restoring ecological function can be achieved by simply replicating historical form, or if new forms or processes must be engaged to improve or regenerate ecological conditions. A common example of rehabilitating a site to improve ecological conditions is the removal of existing invasive plants and replanting with appropriate plant species that will proliferate in contemporary site conditions and will support desired ecological processes.

Often opportunities exist to add design elements that draw attention to restoration actions, such as integrating gateways, paths, markers and art pieces into the design of the site. Such marking and features for human interaction foster awareness of human care and place attachment, which in turn can attract additional public appreciation and stewardship of a site.

Name: The Cedar River Watershed Education Center

Location: Cedar Falls, Washington, USA

Date: 2001

Designer: Jones & Jones

Located on a disturbed site in a protected watershed, The Cedar River Watershed Education Center re-established ecological function to the site while providing over 900m^2 (10,000 square feet) of educational facility.

←

Name: Ravenna Creek daylighting project

Location: Seattle, Washington USA

Date: 2006

Designer: Gaynor Inc

Formerly piped, this creek daylighting project returned 200 metres (650 feet) of creek channel back to the surface, re-establishing it as native habitat.

Creating high-performance landscapes

When historic conditions have been degraded or need to be replaced, certain ecological functions can still be re-established in landscapes. These design actions should strive to achieve high ecological performance, often by serving multiple functions. The design of these high-performance landscapes will likely look very different from historical conditions, but may replace or regenerate lost or degraded functions in the same system or watershed. They might also create habitat for species suited to the new conditions. The high-performance landscape can also provide significant ecological services such as water retention and cleansing. In addition to supplying direct ecological services, high-performance landscapes may support an improved quality of life in dense urban settlements, reducing the human carbon footprint associated with sprawl, and cultivate the stewardship needed to maintain a landscape over time.

↙↓
....
Name: MFO Park

Location: Neu Oerlikon, Zurich, Switzerland

Date: 2002

Designer: Burckhardt + Partner AG and Raderschall Landschaftsarchitekten

This six-storey trellis structure forms a new kind of park in a former office district that is now a high-density residential neighbourhood. With diverse vines growing on the multi-layered structure, the park supplies insect habitat, stormwater attenuation and heat island reduction. It also provides exciting active and passive recreational opportunities for residents.

Designing for ecosystem health and biodiversity

Effective design intended to foster diversity and ecosystem integrity requires knowledge of the local ecosystem's components and interactions. While there is typically insufficient detailed information about a particular system available to the landscape architect, there are some general principles from which to work:

→ 1) Consider the various spatial scales of ecosystems and their interactions, from global to the very immediate, and for both the desired flows (connected habitat) and potential impacts (invasion from exotics) between scales.

→ 2) First, protect the biological integrity and function that exists; it is much more difficult to restore ecosystems than to maintain existing ones.

→ 3) Prioritize protection and restoration of water habitats and their edges. Wetlands, estuaries and the riparian margins of stream and river corridors harbour the most diverse assemblies of plant and wildlife species.

→ 4) Use the known requirements of keystone or representative species or habitats as guides. Use existing 'reference' habitats, but consider time, process and successional stages when planning.

→ 5) Know your site and the specific opportunities and challenges it presents to successful establishment over time. For example, undesired 'exotic' canopy species can be used to shelter native species until they are established, and then removed later.

→ 6) Apply the principles of landscape ecology, adapting them to your specific situation (see Chapter 3).

→ 7) Work in teams with scientists who have the required expertise. Landscape architects are often the best leaders of interdisciplinary teams, as they are able to join scientific knowledge with human needs.

→ 8) Cultivate opportunities for human interaction and the stewardship that will be required to maintain new landscapes. Highlight the opportunities for human health, democratic access and engagement with diverse cultural communities.

←

Name: The Cedar River Watershed Education Center

Location: Cedar Falls, Washington, USA

Date: 2001

Designer: Jones & Jones

The campus design of this environmental learning centre is integrated into its surroundings, both visually and functionally, in a high-performance landscape that filters stormwater and provides a diversity of habitat types while serving the educational mission of the centre.

In order to effectively interact with a project through its design and implementation, it is helpful to understand the sequence and interrelated structure of typical project phases. The framework provided in this section is inclusive of the standard activities required to develop, design, implement, maintain and learn from an ecological design project, and highlights the iterative relationships of these project phases.

While there is a general progression to the stages of the framework, steps can be taken to return to a particular phase to update conditions as they become more explicit or change over time.

The following sections provide detailed information about each of the phases. Many are combined as the relationships between phases are important for progressing through the design process. For example, there is always a strong link between design and construction, as the quality and clarity of the landscape architect's design and construction documents influence a building contractor's performance.

Goals | Objectives

Establishing the goals and objectives for a project is paramount in determining the scope and development of how the project will proceed. Goals are typically defined by general categories such as increasing biodiversity, improving upon existing ecological processes or habitat conditions, or managing the impacts of stormwater for a particular project. Objectives are more specific and often quantifiable descriptions that are developed to achieve the overall goals of a project. For example, project goals established to reduce overall stormwater runoff and improve water quality may set objectives for the retention and/or detention of a certain percentage of the runoff generated on a site, to remove certain pollutants from water that flows from or through a site. Often, such goals and objectives are mandated by regulation and must be identified early in the project.

While these two phases of the design framework are often developed early in the design process, the iterative structure of the framework suggests that goals and objectives for any given project be continually re-evaluated as a project progresses, and site conditions and constituent desires are better understood and developed.

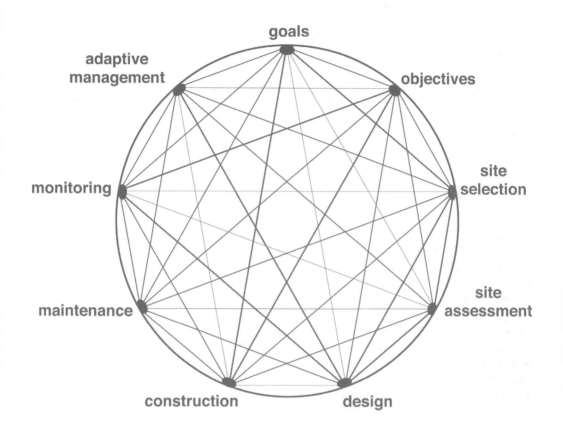

↑

Name: Project structure

Source: Susan Buis and Linda Krippner

This framework is inclusive of the standard activities required to develop, design, implement, maintain and learn from an ecological design project. It also highlights the iterative relationships of these project phases.

Site selection | Assessment

Selecting a site is an important component of the overall design process, yet is often limited by the scope and location of a particular project. When mitigating against possible negative effects from a particular project – as may be legally required – an off-project-site may be most appropriate for creating or restoring habitat or ecological processes to compensate for project impacts. Typically, off-site mitigation areas are selected as near to the project site as possible and within the same watershed. The option to conduct off-site mitigation is typically determined by the jurisdiction or agency that manages environmental conditions for a particular area. Regardless of the site selected, a thorough assessment of the site is required to comprehend both constraints to and potential for incorporating ecological design practices, whether for the protection, restoration, enhancement or creation of ecological processes.

↗

Name: Allegheny Riverfront Park

Location: Pittsburgh, Pennsylvania, USA

Date: 1994–1998

Designer: Michael Van Valkenburgh Associates, Inc

To ensure that the goals and objectives of a project are met and that the construction process doesn't degrade the environment, it is important for the landscape architect to develop construction documents that are of high quality; appropriate construction practices must be employed.

Design | Construction

Much of this book has focused on theory and design strategies associated with ecological design practices. However, as the illustrated framework reveals, the development of a design represents only one phase of the design process. Yet this phase in the framework is critical in that it unites the goals and objectives of a particular project with the realities of site conditions and processes, and coalesces them into a functional and meaningful design. This is where the visionary elements of a project's structure are proposed, vetted and developed as a detailed set of interacting systems and elements, taken through several design phases from conceptual and schematic ideas into documents that can be used for construction.

Typically, ecological projects are designed and detailed by a diverse team of consultants, including and often led by the landscape architect. The quality and accuracy of the construction documents are critical in carrying the design team's intent through to the initial completed landscape.

The connecting line between the design and construction phases in the ecological design framework reveals one of the strongest and most iterative connections in the process. The phase of construction is the physical realization of the design on the site, and if not properly implemented the process of construction can inflict considerable damage through excess site disturbance, soil compaction, erosion, and vegetation and topsoil damage. There must be continual discussion between those designing and those constructing a site in order for a project to be adapted to discovered site conditions while still maintaining the integrity of the original design goals.

→
....
Name: Union Bay Natural Area

Location: Seattle, Washington, USA

Owner: University of Washington

The selection and assessment of a site is important to the overall design process. This natural area and associated wetlands have been selected for restoration to offset or mitigate the impacts created by a nearby transportation project.

Maintenance | Monitoring

Maintenance is a critical component of any ecological design project. As discussed in previous chapters, the biological and physical conditions of a site are never static; they are emerging over time as plants grow, seasons change, and contextual conditions evolve. Establishing and implementing a maintenance plan better enables the continued ecological operation and management of a site. Maintenance actions may include regular checks and cleaning required for a water flow system to operate effectively, or the continued clearing of invasive species on a site to allow for intended species to establish and proliferate.

Closely associated with continued maintenance is the development and implementation of a monitoring plan that collects information on the effectiveness of design, maintenance and management actions. A monitoring plan requires a systematic approach to evaluating site conditions that tests design assumptions and informs management strategies. Specific examination of a project's performance enables the design team and end user to learn from the project and to understand what and how specific aspects of a project work, which will then determine whether a project is meeting its performance goals and objectives.

↓→
....

Name: Monitoring performance

Location: Snohomish, Washington, USA

Designer: Snyder Roofing of Washington, LLC

Monitoring project performance following construction is important for all ecological design projects. It enables the design team to learn from and adapt the project if necessary in order to meet goals and objectives, while providing a better understanding for application and performance on other projects.

Adaptive management

An adaptive management approach incorporates research into the ecological design framework through the integration of design, monitoring and management to systematically test assumptions about design elements in order to learn and then to adapt management actions.

The evaluation of a project's operations is developed through consistent monitoring to determine if a project is functioning at an optimal capacity to meet goals and objectives. If it is determined that a project is not performing adequately, the information generated enables a project team to adapt management and design structures to maximize the potential of site and project.

This flexibility in long-term management has multiple benefits in that it increases the likelihood that the ecological conditions of a site will be enhanced; it promotes active engagement and site stewardship; and it offers an opportunity for the design team and stakeholders in the project to learn from design and management actions.

Learning about site responses to active and passive forms of manipulation allows the landscape architect and the profession to avoid making the same mistakes in subsequent projects while at the same time maximizing and building upon successes. The information gained from this work informs the management direction and actions for the project in question while also establishing a precedent for future work.

Civic participation can be a key ingredient to advancing and maintaining ecological projects throughout their lives. In particular, public involvement can be critical in supporting projects in their initial phases, in participating in conceptual and schematic design phases, and in helping to create and steward a built landscape in the long term.

Project advocacy roles

In the first phase of a project, citizen advocacy is often the catalyst for project conceptualization and in raising funds to sponsor or initiate a project. For example, neighbourhood residents advocated retaining New York's High Line as an amenity for several years before the city established policy to retain rather than demolish the structure. Citizens participated in meetings, helped to sponsor a design competition, and lobbied the city to find innovative ways to preserve and repurpose the structure as an urban park. Often, landscape architects assist with citizen advocacy groups, contributing meaningful public service.

Participation in planning and design processes

Participation by public and institutional advocates is also invaluable during the design process to ensure that the design is responsive to the current and future needs of diverse user groups. Citizens are particularly helpful in establishing planning and design goals and objectives, and in responding to design alternatives. Citizens can directly contribute their project ideas in design charrettes – participatory events led by design professionals that can draw upon local knowledge and talent. Landscape architects who are skilled at eliciting input, listening to multiple voices, and then responding to public concerns and aspirations in their design solutions are more likely to find successful acceptance of their project proposals. This is not to say that landscape architects should not bring their own creativity and informed ideas to the design process, but that the ideas can be inspired, refined and made more relevant by engaging the public in the process.

←

Name: Project Advocacy

Location: Taipei, Taiwan

Source: Jeff Hou

Students and activists from SAVE International staged a skit in front of the Taipei Train Station to draw attention to the plight of the black-faced spoonbill whose habitat was threatened by a proposed steel and petrochemical plant on the southwest coast of Taiwan. The project has since been terminated, and the habitat is now a protected wildlife area.

→

Name: Participation in the design process

Location: Seattle, Washington, USA

At a neighbourhood planning workshop citizens arranged blocks over an aerial photograph to explore options for increased density and pedestrian amenities in their new town centre.

Participation in the construction process

In many cases, citizens can also participate in the construction of a public landscape design. While the level of participation depends upon the owning agency and construction contract structure, non-profit organizations and public-private partnerships between governmental agencies and non-governmental groups can be effective in attracting volunteer labour to help build a community-based project. It is important that citizens be given safe tasks where they can successfully collaborate and execute; training is often necessary. Planting parties where volunteers learn appropriate soil preparation and plant installation methods have double benefits of accomplishing the work while educating participants. Non-profit and university design-build programmes can wholly complete small landscape-based projects, sometimes also involving the public.

Participation in stewardship and monitoring

When the public has been involved in the design and/or construction processes, they are more likely to invest in a project and to provide care and long-term stewardship of a landscape. While volunteers should not be relied upon for primary responsibility of landscape maintenance, they can provide critical assistance in eliminating invasive plant species, overseeing appropriate park use, and monitoring ecological conditions. Annual bird, fish and insect counts that engage trained volunteers can assist biologists in assessing the ecological health of a landscape, as can students and citizens who monitor water quality and biotic richness.

↑→
....
Name: Skyway Park

Location: Skyway, Washington, USA

Date: 2009

Designer: University of Washington, Design|Build Programme

Undergraduate students in the Design|Build Programme at the University of Washington work with local communities to identify, design and construct projects as part of their required curriculum. This project provides a central meeting area within the park, featuring an open-sided shelter with a green roof and seating areas.

Participatory design methods

The landscape architect employs a range of participatory methods in the design process. Listening and goal-setting meetings, workshops, design charrettes and priority-setting forums are all useful formats through the planning and design phases. Online surveys and participatory techniques to gather local knowledge and preferences are also useful, particularly when they involve spatial marking on maps, or display clear design alternatives for public feedback. It is essential that broad outreach to diverse constituents is done, reaching various age and income groups and targeting those who are most affected by the project. This outreach is typically done by the client agency at the behest of the design team.

Graphic representations of project processes, timelines, potential site configurations and simulations of how the site might function and appear are important tools that the landscape architect uses to engage the public. While static two-dimensional drawings and three-dimensional models are traditionally relied upon, video and real-time three-dimensional drawings are increasingly used. Tools that enable active spatial manipulation by workshop participants, such as the use of Lego and blocks in envisioning neighbourhood building and open-space massing, are also effective in soliciting meaningful public participation.

As indicated in the project implementation framework, most ecological projects require significant maintenance and stewardship to ensure their success over time. Below, we elaborate on the role of the landscape architect during this critical phase for project success.

Stewardship plans

Landscape architects are increasingly producing stewardship plans that clearly describe the design intent of their built projects. These plans provide maintenance protocols as well as standards and measures that can be used to assess the success of management actions over time. If a project is legally mandated, such as mitigation for lost wetland habitats, maintenance and monitoring may be required for several years. In such cases, the design team will produce a set of maintenance and monitoring guidelines that the landscape architect or owner's representative can use in order to check that procedures are being followed.

Without communicating the original goals and vision, a landscape project is extremely vulnerable to change that may inadvertently cause its failure or, bit by bit, unravel its design identity. While in many cases adaptive management is required for a project to succeed ecologically, management decisions can unintentionally weaken its overall success. Alternatively, the provision and use of a stewardship plan and continued involvement of the landscape architect can be directed to strengthen the design concept and can greatly facilitate appropriate adaptive management decisions.

←↑
....
Name: Herring's House Park

**Location: Seattle,
Washington, USA**

Date: 2001

**Designer: J A Brennan
Associates**

Landscape architect J A
Brennan created a new intertidal salt marsh from a previous
industrial site on the Duwamish
River. The firm then produced a
Stewardship and Adaptive
Management Plan for the park
that included original design
intent, conditions observed in
post-construction analysis,
potential improvements, and a
schedule for regularly monitoring
the park's ecological and public
use conditions over the first
three years of its establishment.

Long-term stewardship and participation

Long-term public involvement in stewardship
is usually necessary for the ecological and
social success of a project. As described
previously, public commitment to long-term
stewardship can be instigated in the design
phase through effective public participation
processes. It can also be cultivated through
a meaningful, aesthetic and functional
project that engenders attachment and
caring, and this is largely under the aegis of
the landscape architect's design and the
successful execution of the project.

The winning competition entry for the 2001 Freshkills Park design proposed the concept of 'Lifescape' – a process designed to regenerate the dynamics and biological diversity of the site. To be built on New York's Staten Island over what was formerly the world's largest landfill, the design intends to transform the 890-hectare (2,200-acre) site into a park that restores diverse landscape ecologies while offering a wide range of recreational, educational and cultural opportunities. In addition to enhancing existing wetlands, waterways and lowlands, the design proposes to regenerate historically diverse ecologies of the site, including native eastern prairie, woodlands, swamp-forest, bog, tidal salt marsh and a mixture of forest and meadow habitats that will crest the landfill mounds and frame vistas of the surrounding landscape.

The competition team proposed a matrix of 'lines (threads), surfaces (mats) and clusters (islands)' to promote access and movement of both people and biota through the site, while constructing a self-sustaining landscape that will be ecologically robust enough to accommodate change over time, yet maintain its overall identity and high level of ecological performance.

The site will be interwoven with an intricate interconnected circulation system within and outside its boundaries, linking both ecologies and facilities. It will be richly programmed and developed for diverse recreation including biking, nature trails, horseback riding, skating, kayaking, fishing, birdwatching, ball and field sports, nature education, gardens, picnicking, restaurants, an open-air market, a visitor centre, and large-scale public art. The development of five separate areas of the park – The Confluence, North Park, South Park, East Park and West Park, each with a distinct character and programming approach – will be phased over the next 30 years, recognizing the dynamic nature of the project.

Ecological approaches:
→ Restoration of diverse ecologies: prairie, wetlands, forests, tidal salt marsh
→ Commitment to renewable and sustainable technologies
→ Flexible adaptive management approach
→ Robust and diverse interconnected facilities and recreational opportunities
→ Methane gas from the landfill harvested and used to heat nearby homes

Project processes
← Stewardship **Freshkills Park**

←↙↓

Name: Freshkills Park

Location: Staten Island, New York, USA

Date: 2006–

Designer: James Corner Field Operations

In the previous chapters we have learned that the processes that form, regulate and regenerate ecological conditions in a landscape are complex and vary through time and in space. This understanding enables us to develop design approaches that may enhance ecological processes on a site. It also introduces the potential to reduce off-site impacts by increasing the efficiency of energy and water use, reducing waste and emphasizing the generation and use of renewable energy sources. This approach to design is process based.

Designers often use metaphors to better grasp and convey these processes and often-complex issues. Metaphors are particularly important in the conceptual visioning of a design idea, and often serve as a descriptive link that unites process and form. Ecological design employs action-based metaphors that describe the operation of a particular design or process.

In this chapter, we have selected several terms that metaphorically, as well as literally, describe some common design operations employed in the field of ecological design. Supported by case study examples, each set of operations is described in form and process to indicate how it functions in a design to achieve a particular goal or design objective.

←↖
....
Name: Hammarby Sjostad Neighbourhood

Location: Stockholm, Sweden

Date: 1992

Designer: City of Stockholm, Stockholm Water, Birka Energy

Sustainable and ecological operations are employed throughout this waterfront neighbourhood slated for 10,000 dwellings. Practices include stormwater harvest and filtration, compact housing interlaced with useable green spaces and connections to Stockholm via transit and cycle paths.

Echoing the 'Rethink – Reuse – Recycle' idiom, this operation presents a spectrum of actions that are aimed at preserving ecological and human resources. It is important in any system that exhibits ecological integrity to protect that landscape from degradation, given the challenge and length of time that it takes for any system to reach and maintain its integral biodiversity and point of healthy dynamic equilibrium. Policies and practices that establish land protection boundaries for valued ecosystems, and which prevent erosion, pollution and exotic species invasion at the source are paramount in ecological planning and design.

Designs that conserve and reuse material resources in their construction phase are meant to protect landscapes by reducing impacts from forestry, mining, excavation and transport. Similarly, reuse of site resources in ongoing site operations over time can reduce demand for limited off-site resources, such as collection of stormwater for irrigation reuse. For example, in Melbourne, Australia, stormwater is harvested from the surrounding buildings and streets, treated in a series of three urban wetlands, and then stored in underground cisterns where it supplies over 80 per cent of the irrigation for the 2.5-hectare (6-acre) Melbourne Docklands Park.

Brooklyn Bridge Park

Brooklyn Bridge Park is an example of extensive large-scale material reuse. Stretching along the eastern harbour in the Brooklyn Borough of New York City, the design's reuse of site structures and local materials in this post-industrial park has been driven by a structural economy, not only reducing resource use, but also conserving funds so that the park can be constructed within constrained budgets.

The park design calls for repurposing six former industrial marine piers including retaining building skeletons to shelter and define play areas, and reusing steel columns and masts for lighting poles. Where a portion of a pier has been removed, fields of marine pilings have been maintained for textural qualities, iconic memory and marine habitat.

Thousands of metres of yellow pine timbers from a former storage building have been recycled for use in new decking, structures and site furnishings. Salvaged granite blocks from a local bridge project form a new amphitheatre with sweeping views across the East River and New York Harbour, and tens of thousands of cubic metres of fill material excavated in a nearby transportation project are being used to shape the new promontories and undulating landscapes on Pier 1 and upland portions of the park.

CASE STUDY

Ecological approaches:
→ Material reuse

→ 2.5 hectares (six acres) of diverse habitat

→ Native plantings

→ New public shoreline access

→ Stormwater collected and reused

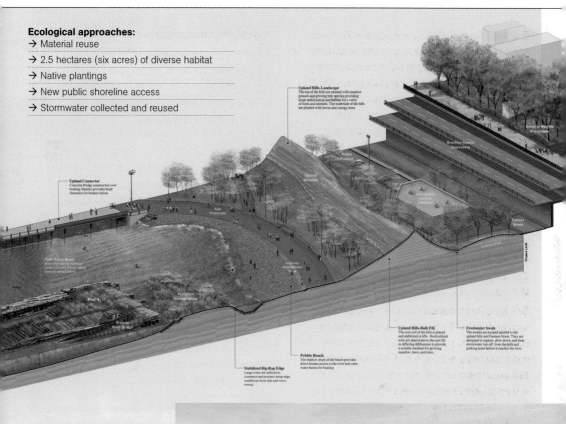

Upland Hills-Landscape
The top of the hills are planted with meadow grasses and growing tree species providing slope stabilization and habitat for a variety of birds and animals. The waterside of the hills are planted with lawns and canopy trees.

Upland Connector
Concrete bridge constructed over boating channel provides head clearance for boaters below.

Upland Hills-Bulk Fill
The core soil of the hills is placed and stabilized in lifts. Horticultural soils are placed above the core fill in differing thicknesses to provide a suitable medium for growing meadow, lawn, and trees.

Freshwater Swale
The swales are located parallel to the upland hills and Furman Street. They are designed to capture, slow down, and treat stormwater run-off from the hills and parking areas before it reaches the river.

Pebble Beach
The shallow slope of the beach provides direct human access to the river and calm water basins for boating

Stabilized Rip Rap Edge
Large rocks are utilized to construct and protect steep edge conditions from tide and wave energy

↑→
Name: Brooklyn Bridge Park

Location: Brooklyn, New York, west of the Brooklyn-Queens Expressway

Date: 2010

Designer: Michael Van Valkenburgh Associates

CASE STUDY

A common definition of scaffold is a temporary structure used to support people and material in the construction or repair of buildings and other large structures. In the context of ecological design, the metaphor of scaffold is used similarly in that it signifies the creation of a structure or set of actions that enable and initiate ecological processes to progress on a site or in a particular system.

As the processes are reformed, and as they become more viable and sustainable enough to achieve a particular goal or objective in a design, the scaffold assumes a role of lesser importance. The applications of this concept in design are far-reaching. For example, scaffold can be used to describe a particular seed mix designed to stabilize and improve conditions of the soil for a future community of plants. Scaffold can also be a weir across a stream channel that serves as temporary structure for maintaining a stream bed, enhancing habitat conditions for fish and other aquatic species.

Oriental Bay

Working closely with engineers, coastal engineers and the City of Wellington in New Zealand, the Isthmus Group developed a design for Oriental Bay in downtown Wellington that serves local recreational requirements while enhancing ecological conditions. Originally built in the mid-1800s from ship ballast, the beach along Oriental Bay was constantly eroding, continually requiring new sand to be brought in to supplement that which was lost.

While early design conceptions called for a broad swathe of beach, the design that Isthmus and Architecture Workshop developed divides the one-kilometre (half-mile) beach into three smaller reaches to respect the crenellated character of the existing inner city bay and the surrounding landscape forms. In order to reduce the rate of beach erosion and maintain the character of the area, the local coastal processes were modelled and three distinct sea structures were designed to control sand drift.

While structurally independent, the sea structures are arranged to support coastal processes and enable the re-establishment of a nearshore ecosystem within the bay. The most visible of these structures is an abstracted headland of precast, stacked concrete slabs that extends into the bay, emulating a coastal reef and its aquatic substrate functions. Since the project was constructed, bright green algae has grown on the surface of the concrete slabs in the intertidal zone, which now supports a diverse array of molluscs and other invertebrate marine species.

Ecological approaches:
→ Provides habitat for marine species
→ Protects and preserves existing trees along the waterfront
→ Manages and controls stormwater runoff to reduce beach erosion
→ Provides places for the public to access the waterfront

←↑

Name: Oriental Bay

Location: Wellington, New Zealand

Date: 2001

Designer: Isthmus and Architecture Workshop

A catalyst can initiate or increase the rate of change in a system. In this operation, the landscape architect proposes actions that are meant to initiate self-sustaining processes.

Once begun, the progression of these processes can restore or regenerate a site over time, though often with human intervention to guide or direct a trajectory towards a desired ecologically healthy state. Examples are planting 'pioneer' or 'neophyte' species such as those that fix nitrogen or build soil quality; introduction of water to a landscape, such as rainwater to wetland areas; creation of landforms that will collect or regulate water, such as landscape depressions, ridges, and tidal terraces; and social processes that inspire human activism, community building and long-term stewardship of landscapes.

In regenerating ecological landscapes, plants that are native to a particular region are typically selected as they are more likely to sustain related food networks of local animal species. However, in situations where natives would not survive or be slower to establish, non-invasive exotics can be useful in establishing supportive growing conditions.

Magnuson Park Wetlands

At Magnuson Park in Seattle the designers aimed to initiate the processes of establishing quality amphibian and avian habitat on a former naval airstrip while also upgrading park recreational fields. The design team established a hydrological regime that favours the native Pacific Chorus frog (*Hyla regilla*), which requires water for most – but not all – of the year. Its exotic predator, the bullfrog (*Rana catesbeiana*) needs flooded year-round habitat.

To accomplish this regime, the new wetlands were formed as a grid of cell depressions arranged in a pattern that tilts from one side to the other across the site. In the rainy season, treated stormwater runoff from the ball fields and parking lots fill the depressions, first flooding the cells on the highest side until they flow over low berm weirs into the next lowest cells, and so on.

As seasonal rains subside and the Pacific Chorus frogs migrate to upland forest habitat, the lower cells begin to dry up, making conditions inhospitable for the predator bullfrog. The berms, cell interiors and forest habitat were planted with diverse native species, with the expectation that other species will colonize the site over time. Strategically placed logs and snags provide shelter for insects and amphibians and perching and nesting sites for birds.

CASE STUDY

Ecological approaches:

→ Utilizes clean stormwater to generate amphibian habitat

→ Cleaned water from research lab used to sustain wetland

→ Snags and downed logs for bird, insect and amphibian habitat

→ 26-hectare (65-acre) wetland complex will include a freshwater lagoon

→ Trails and educational platforms

→ Extensive use of compost and on-site biomass

↑↗→

Name: Magnuson Park Wetlands

Location: Seattle, Washington, USA

Date: 2009

Designer: The Berger Partnership and Sheldon Associates

To stratify refers to the process of forming, arranging, or depositing layers. As an operative metaphor in ecological design, stratify refers to increasing the resiliency and strength of a system or design to respond to change. This metaphor describes several design approaches. The first is a physical stratification or layering of design elements in space that engage distinct components of an ecological system. The second form of metaphor refers to the process of layering that supports redundancy, an important tool in designing for increased resilience in a site or system (see Chapter 3). In this regard, redundancy in form and process enables a site to adapt and evolve in the event of collapse or degradation of a particular system. As described in the following case study, the Underwood Family Sonoran Landscape Laboratory utilizes multiple sources of water to meet the irrigation requirements of the diverse matrix of habitat types supported by the design of the garden.

Underwood Family Sonoran Landscape Laboratory

In 2007, the College of Architecture and Landscape Architecture (CALA) at the University of Arizona completed a new expansion facility that operates as an outdoor laboratory and demonstration facility for sustainable design practices in the arid southwest of the United States. Nestled between the new facility and a parking lot, the landscape architect – in collaboration with other design, engineering, and irrigation professionals working on the project – specifically focused on incorporating and showcasing water-conscious design solutions through the approximately 0.5-hectare (1-acre) site.

The integrated design reveals a stratified approach to water harvesting that utilizes a range of available sources such as roof and parking lot runoff, cooling condensate from the building's air conditioning system, and grey water from the drinking fountains. These sources combine to dramatically reduce water consumption for irrigation purposes and focuses attention towards capturing, detaining and maximizing the utilization of available water sources. Approximately 870,000 litres (230,000 gallons) of water are harvested annually from these sources. Once the plantings for the site are established, this amount of water harvest should meet the needs of the site resulting in a self-sustaining landscape.

CASE STUDY

Operations

Ecological approaches:

→ Passive and active water harvesting

→ Creation of 0.5 hectare (1-acre) of a diverse range of regionally endemic habitats

→ Creates a cooler microclimate

→ Incorporates educational guidelines

←↑

Name: Underwood Family Sonoran Landscape Laboratory

Location: The University of Arizona, Tucson, USA

Date: 2007

Designer: Ten Eyck Landscape Architects, Inc

Often the ecological designer attempts to regulate or control flows across the urban landscape. The use of landscape forms to control such flows might be intended to contain impacts of a design to the project site; compensate for or protect against adverse impacts of alterations elsewhere in the system; concentrate energy or materials (such as water or nutrients) for their life-giving properties or to cleanse them; or to store resources for later use. For example, in Waitangi Park on Wellington harbour in New Zealand (see page 17), urban stormwater is collected in subsurface wetlands where it is cleansed through microbial action on the gravel substrate and roots of wetland plants, and then stored in an open lagoon cistern for reuse in irrigating the park. The wetlands that the collected stormwater support also provide habitat and aesthetic benefits.

Scharnhauser Park Housing

At Scharnhauser Park Housing in Germany, a new linear park stretching between refurbished barracks functions as a rainwater collector, flood control device, public space and play area. Stormwater runoff is directed into a series of infiltration terraces where it is temporarily detained and filtered and feeds underground streams. Any overflow cascades across the terraced landscape in a dramatic 1.5-kilometre-long (1-mile) waterfall.

Runoff that infiltrates the soil feeds the groundwater table, with excess filling ponds at the bottom of the system that further contain and treat the stormwater and provide wetland wildlife habitat. In addition, residents capture rainwater in tanks and hold and infiltrate it through permeable surfaces such as bioswales, roof gardens and parking areas.

By controlling the hydrologic regime, collecting, containing and infiltrating water on the site, sanitary sewer overflows and river flooding downstream are reduced in a cost-effective manner. The green ribbons of visible stormwater infrastructure unite the housing development in signature multi-functional public spaces that bring attention to the powerful role of water in the landscape.

CASE STUDY

Ecological approaches:

→ Integrated open spaces

→ Adaptive reuse of former military housing barracks

→ Dense housing serves diverse residents

→ Low-energy buildings with photovoltaics and geothermal sources

→ Light rail transportation to city centre, pedestrian priority streets and limited parking spaces

→ Water management and cleansing through landscape features

↑↗→

Name: Scharnhauser Park Housing

Location: Ostfildern, Germany

Date: 1996–2003

Designer: Janson + Wofrum Architektur + Stadtplanung and Atelier Dreiseitl

A sieve is used to separate or filter elements of a material or mixture. In ecological design, the concept of a sieve is often used to describe the process of cleansing water of unwanted material and the more insidious components of chemical pollution. Wetlands and the ecological processes they support cleanse water naturally by slowing the flow to allow sediments to drop from the water column, and enabling the capacity that many plants have for absorbing toxins or heavy metals in their tissues.

Porous and permeable substrates also operate as filters by enabling water to drain through the interstitial spaces of the soil while capturing pollutants. The sieve concept, incorporating wetland processes and permeability, is common approach to improving the water quality of a site and extended landscape conditions. It is often employed through a variety of structures and mechanisms, such as the process of capturing and filtering stormwater, and the biological treatment of wastewater.

Shanghai Houtan Park

Built on a narrow 14-hectare (35-acre), formerly industrial site on the Huangpu River waterfront in Shanghai, China, Houtan Park was initially designed to demonstrate green technologies for a World Expo event in Shanghai and has since transitioned into a permanent public waterfront park. Partnering with students from the nearby Peking University Graduate School of Landscape Architecture, the landscape architect employed strategies that are regenerative and designed to improve the ecological health of the adjacent river and parklands.

This regenerative approach is completed through the design of a constructed wetland that flows 1.7 kilometres (1 mile) through the site, reinvigorating the waterfront and cleansing contaminated water from the adjacent Huangpu River (see diagram on opposite page). Variations in the elevations of the wetlands create cascades and terraces that oxygenate the nutrient-rich waters and enable sediments to settle out of the water column. Select species of plants known to absorb chemicals and other pollutants were installed along the entire length of the wetland. Initial field testing has shown a dramatic improvement in the quality of water as it moves through the system, making it safe for all uses except human consumption.

The combination of channel structure and plants serve as an effective sieve, filtering unwanted sediments and pollutants and improving the overall quality of the water, while also reducing the financial commitments required of the city to cleanse the water through conventional treatment practices.

CASE STUDY

Ecological approaches:

→ Constructed wetland to cleanse polluted waters

→ Ecological approach to flood control

→ Reclamation of existing industrial structures and materials

→ Integration of urban agriculture

↑↓

Name: **Shanghai Houtan Park**

Location: **Shanghai, China**

Date: **2010**

Designer: **Turenscape**

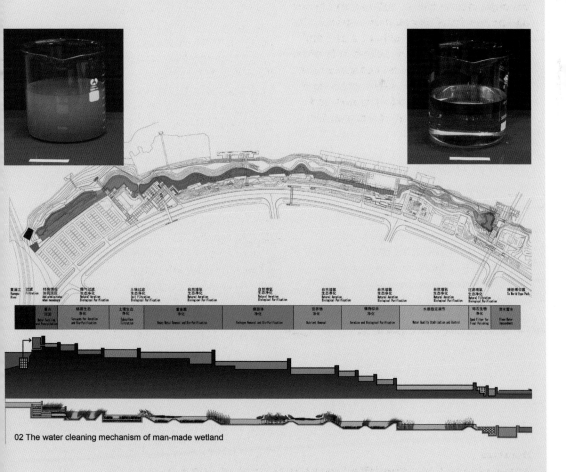

02 The water cleaning mechanism of man-made wetland

To metabolize means to digest and convert material into energy. Given supporting conditions, the inherent life processes of plants and soil microorganisms and microbes can metabolize, break down and sequester environmental toxins, and thereby transform polluted sites into healthy ones.

Through populating sites with species that are known for their bioremediation capabilities, landscape architects can employ living organisms to remediate the ground and waters of low to moderately polluted brownfield sites. Poplars and willows can uptake, break down and volatize petroleum hydrocarbons, nutrients and metals; microbes in compost and on the roots of wetland plants such as reeds and cattails degrade and transform pollutants such as fuels and solvents; sunflowers and mustard family plants are known to uptake and sequester heavy metals; and fungi and their mycelia in soil are able to rapidly digest hydrocarbons in petroleum products such as oil and pesticides.

While herbaceous plants, compost and constructed wetlands are useful in shallow soil situations, deeper rooting trees can reach contaminants lower in the soil profile. Integration of planting and soil inoculation strategies into the design of post-industrial sites and cities can harness ecological processes to remediate sites over time, while also exhibiting to the public that these positive progressions are taking place.

Landscape Park Duisburg-Nord

On the site of a former steel manufacturing plant in Germany's Ruhr Valley, landscape architects Latz + Partner encountered a landscape of industrial ruins, slag heaps and soils polluted by hydrocarbons and heavy metals slated to be transformed into a public park. The landscape was comprised of an intact collection of diverse structures and a site rich in pioneering plant species, some rare, that had established on the nutrient-poor slag heaps, ore piles and contaminated ground.

By retaining the remnant industrial structures and infrastructure patterns of the former steel plant, Latz + Partner intended to interpret the site's unique qualities while transforming the structures to function anew as artful places of play and creativity. While the most heavily polluted areas were capped or sequestered from public access, the neophyte plantings became part of the site recovery strategy and were recognized as one of the site's many potential inherent palimpsests that could help tell the story of this post-industrial landscape.

New trees, meadows and gardens are fitted between the structures and walls of the industrial relics. Today, over half a million people visit the park yearly, to bicycle throughout its 230 hectares (570 acres), practice on the climbing walls of the old ore bunkers, dive in the Gasometer (a huge former gas tank), attend events in the exhibition hall and plaza, stroll along the elevated rail line and the now-clean waters of the canal, and enjoy the intricate bunker gardens from an elevated catwalk.

CASE STUDY

Ecological approaches:

→ Phyto and bio-remediation of minimally contaminated soils and water

→ Separation and capping of heavily contaminated water and soil

→ Extensive repurposing of industrial structures

→ Link in system of Ruhr Valley remediated post-industrial sites

←↖↑

Name: Landscape Park Duisburg-Nord

Location: Duisburg, Ruhr Valley, Germany

Date: 2002

Designer: Latz + Partner

The definition of mimic is to copy or imitate closely. Used metaphorically in ecological design, one application of mimic is the process of replicating biological adaptations to changing conditions. Termed biomimicry, it is an approach to design that examines and emulates biological structures and processes to meet defined goals and design objectives. Applied to landscapes, biomimetic design builds and supports ecological integrity and health. While relatively new to mainstream design practices, biomimicry has been used by many in the past to inform some of the most transformative inventions of our modern era – from the Wright brothers emulating the structure of a vulture's wing to build the first aeroplane, to the barbs on thistle seeds that inspired the design of Velcro®. Biomimicry also takes on different forms in ecological design, such as the capacity to recreate processes or places lost by degradation. In such design cases, model or 'reference' landscapes are often used to identify desired forms, functions and temporal processes that can be emulated in the new landscape.

Cheonggyecheon Stream

Bubbling from the ground in the heart of the central business district in Seoul and then slicing east through the urban grid for 5.8 kilometres (4 miles) before meeting with the Hangang River, the Cheonggyecheon stream project is, to date, one of the most extensive and costly urban stream rehabilitation projects found anywhere in the world. Sponsored by the Seoul Metropolitan Government and completed in 2005, the project removed a major highway through the city and constructed an open channel along the alignment of the historically and culturally important stream corridor. Though the water that flows through the channel is pumped from the Hangang River, the stream corridor successfully integrates open space and mimics landscape forms to create and support terrestrial and aquatic habitat in the downtown core of the city.

Recognizing that a free-flowing stream could not be restored to this highly urban site, the design for the project was founded upon three conceptual axes: history, culture and nature. These axes frame the perspectives of users moving along the stream corridor as the formal structure in the upper reaches of the channel slowly disintegrates into a more natural character. Ecologically, the opening of the stream channel and the reintroduction of water has created a microclimate that is on average nearly 30 degrees (Celsius) cooler than surrounding areas, thereby reducing the urban heat island effect. The new channel supports a diverse array of aquatic and riparian habitats with more than 20 species of fish and 40 species of birds utilizing the corridor.

Ecological approaches:

→ Reconstruction of a historic stream

→ Ecological approach to flood control

→ Provides aquatic and terrestrial habitat

→ Creates a cooler microclimate

←↑

Name: Cheonggyecheon Stream

Location: Seoul, Republic of South Korea

Date: 2005

Designer: Seoul Metropolitan Government

To synthesize commonly refers to the combination or connection of two or more entities. The use of the term synthesis and its derivations in ecological design ranges from the literal definition of the term to more metaphorical concepts of design aggregation or integration. Much like the structure of a system, a synthesis is formed through a composite of integrated elements and relationships to achieve a particular goal or function. For the landscape architect, a design synthesis unites and integrates distinct components of a landscape or site to meet multiple objectives and increase efficiencies. Sites that aggregate multiple functions encourage a diversity of uses and activity, establishing networks of flows that may foster successful urban spaces for both people and wildlife, especially when linked to other places by connecting corridors.

Vancouver Convention Centre West

Located on Vancouver's downtown waterfront, Convention Centre West was designed to weave the natural ecology of the regional environment with the strong form of the surrounding built environment. The project designers developed the building as a model of sustainability, realized through a deeply layered and integrated approach to building and landscape design.

Situated on a 6-hectare (14-acre) former brownfield site, the most visible aspect of the project's embrace of ecological design practices is its 2-hectare (6-acre) living roof with nearly half a million indigenous plants and four bee colonies, providing habitat for birds and insects. The accessible sloping planes that form the roof reflect the mountains of Vancouver Island in the distance and form the end of a continuous series of open spaces, trails and habitats along the city's waterfront. The roof also serves as a primary feature in an innovative conservation and reuse programme within the building that reduces potable water use by up to 70 per cent of other convention centres.

Another feature of ecological importance integrated into the building and site design is an artificial concrete reef that forms an apron extending down from the building and into the intertidal zone of the harbour. Designed in collaboration with marine biologists, the reef functions ecologically as a nearshore environment that supports salmon, crabs, starfish, seaweed and a diverse variety of other marine species. The three aerial images on the right show marine, human and landscape habitats (from top to bottom).

CASE STUDY

Ecological approaches:

→ Waterfront public open spaces, connected to shoreline park system

→ Six-acre (2-hectare) living roof

→ Shoreline and marine habitat enhancement

→ Water conservation and reuse system featuring black water treatment and desalination

→ Extensive use of local and reused materials

→ Natural daylighting and use of sea water to control building temperatures

↙↓

Name: Vancouver Convention Centre West

Location: Vancouver, British Columbia, Canada

Date: 2009

Designer: LMN, MCM + DA Partnership Architecture; PWL Partnership Landscape Architecture

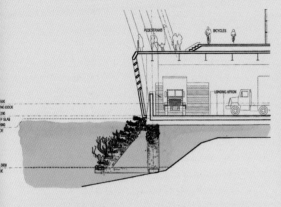

Every landscape contains a narrative of meaning related to its past and present use and function. Ecological landscapes, whether due to their complexity or local indistinctiveness, often require interpretation, emblematic marking or framing to focus attention that will lead to their understanding. Such site-specific comprehension is usually needed to foster appreciation and stewardship. Therefore, the role of design goes beyond catalysing ecological processes, to stimulating human appreciation of the components and functions of ecological landscapes.

A variety of landscape interventions serve to heighten landscape awareness. Landscape markers such as pavilions, sculptures, poles, gateways and nesting boxes attract attention and act as mnemonic devices. Viewpoints and frames can direct attention to particular aspects of a landscape. Immersion in landscapes, in structures such as boardwalks, canopy walks and bridges often inspire human interest and provide memorable points of reference, while art and interesting interpretive devices may compellingly present information and stimulate inquiry about a particular place.

IslandWood Environmental Learning Center

At IslandWood Environmental Learning Center, a series of imaginative teaching and learning places have been carefully sited to focus attention and allow study of numerous representative ecological environments on the 103-hectare (255-acre) site. Serving diverse inner city students as well as local community members, visitors are first introduced to the site at a gateway pavilion before taking the wooded pathways to the Welcome Center, Learning Lab and Residential Lodges; this forest immersion sets the tone for the ensuing experience.

From the central building complex and solar meadow, trails lead to field structures sized for small student groups, including a treehouse overlooking a bog; a floating deck that can be paddled to the centre of a small lake to investigate aquatic organisms; a willow wattle 'blind' with windows for observing birds in the marsh; and a former fire lookout structure that enables study of tree canopy strata and gives an overview of the watershed.

A suspension bridge stretches across the creek ravine for an invigorating perspective of the riparian corridor. Throughout the site and buildings, artwork reflects local geology, flora and fauna. These features in the landscape facilitate a memorable experience, bringing attention to the ecosystem and provoking discovery and learning.

CASE STUDY

Ecological approaches:

→ An extensive environmental analysis determined building and road siting to minimize site impact

→ Teaching Garden with child-sized raised beds and greenhouse

→ Living Machine and constructed wetland used to treat wastewater

→ Passive solar heating of buildings and hot water

→ Demonstration composting toilet

→ Field structures invite immersion in and study of diverse site ecosystems

→ Many materials are salvaged, recycled-sourced or certified as sustainably produced

Name: IslandWood

Location: Bainbridge Island, Washington, USA

Date: 2002

Designer: Mithun and The Berger Partnership

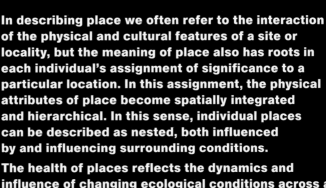

In describing place we often refer to the interaction of the physical and cultural features of a site or locality, but the meaning of place also has roots in each individual's assignment of significance to a particular location. In this assignment, the physical attributes of place become spatially integrated and hierarchical. In this sense, individual places can be described as nested, both influenced by and influencing surrounding conditions.

The health of places reflects the dynamics and influence of changing ecological conditions across a broad range of spatial scales. Ecologically functional streets and parks, added to the responsible design of individual sites, can formulate a community that reduces its resource use, and offers high quality-of-life environments for people and other organisms. Regionally, protected open space systems can provide an economic base and resources for local use as well as habitat for local and migrating species.

This chapter presents an introduction to planned and designed places across a hierarchy of scales, from actively stewarded regions down to individual urban parcels, and illustrates them with exemplary ecological design case studies. Particular planning and design strategies that can be applied at each scale are also described.

←
....
Name: Vancouver Convention Centre and Coal Harbour Waterfront
....
Location: Vancouver, Canada
....
Date: 2009
....
Designer: LMN, PWL and others
....
Vancouver's Coal Harbour Waterfront provides a continuous series of parks, plazas, community facilities and trails that connect to the city's extensive shoreline park and trail system.

All places are part of both a region and a watershed. These two geographic units are often considered the broadest scale at which explicit design and planning strategies are implemented.

Regions

Regions can be defined by similar biophysical characteristics such as landform, climate, biological communities, land uses, and water bodies. For example, the Øresund Region of Denmark and Sweden is organized around the Øresund Sound between the North and Baltic Seas. Regions can also be described in economic, cultural or political terms as in the (San Francisco) Bay Area or as a larger regional example, 'New England'. Bioregional planning and design responds to regional characteristics and patterns and often seeks to emulate, preserve and reestablish representative forms, processes, systems and landscape dynamics such as vegetation, landforms and patterns of water flow.

Watersheds

These are hydrological catchment areas determined by topography that drain to a particular point on the landscape. They can be geographically contained within regional boundaries or extend beyond. Watersheds are hierarchically nested, from the scale of individual parcels to the immense spatial configurations of the Amazon or Nile drainage basins. In this regard, every building roof serves as a catchment area or miniature watershed that feeds a larger system of drainage basins. Therefore, a hierarchy of watersheds can always be identified, from the smallest site to the largest conflation of river systems that drain to a sea.

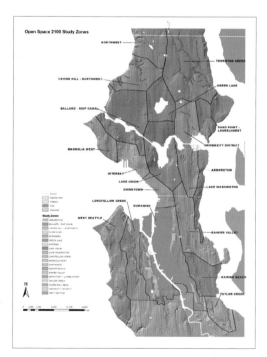

Open Space 2100 Study Zones

←

Name: Cedar River Watershed/Lake Washington Basin

Location: Washington State, USA

Within this region, the city of Seattle sits at the mouths of two watersheds, one of which is the Cedar River/Lake Washington Basin.

←

Name: Seattle watersheds

Location: Seattle, USA

Within Seattle are numerous smaller watershed catchment areas, delineated on this map that landscape architects used to plan connected open spaces for the city.

→

Name: Cascadia

Location: Pacific Northwest, Canada and USA

Designer: Sightline Institute

Cascadia is an international geographic region composed of watersheds draining through the temperate rainforest region of the Pacific Northwest of North America.

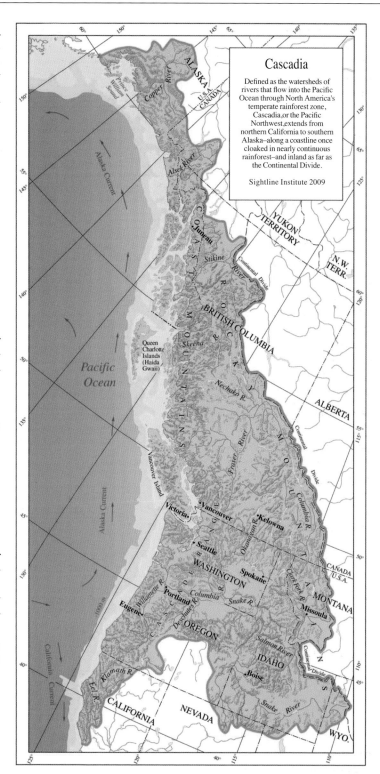

Cascadia

Defined as the watersheds of rivers that flow into the Pacific Ocean through North America's temperate rainforest zone, Cascadia, or the Pacific Northwest, extends from northern California to southern Alaska–along a coastline once cloaked in nearly continuous rainforest–and inland as far as the Continental Divide.

Sightline Institute 2009

Flows + Corridors + Connections

Landscape flows represent processes of movement within and across the landscape. Flows include the movement of water, people, and other species, as well as the energy that is developed, collected, stored, spent and distributed either biologically or chemically. For example, flows may consist of water that moves across the landscape, including the nutrients, minerals, pollutants and life that it carries.

Flows of capital and goods are also typically considered as central to the dynamics of regional conditions. Determining rates, quantities and types of flows is often possible at the regional or watershed scale, providing contextual understanding inputs into a system or site as well as flows emanating from it.

Recognizing flows and their impacts on a system or site enables planners and designers to assess constraints and identify opportunities for corridors and connections as they develop policies, plans and site designs. Such corridors might be fingers of public transport and community development, interlaced with protected greenways, such as those demarcated in Amsterdam and Copenhagen in the 1940s. At an even broader scale, the Rocky Mountains are recognized as a mega-corridor for wildlife; in response, efforts are aimed at preserving contiguous habitat for species that require large open territory for breeding and migration such as the grey wolf and grizzly bear.

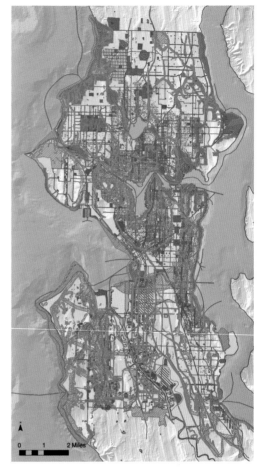

Parks & Community Space   Urban Centers   Water Intervention
Green Transport Corridor   Habitat   Existing Park

↑
....
**Name: Open Space Seattle
2100 Vision**

**Location: Seattle,
Washington, USA**

Date: 2006

**Designer: University of
Washington, Department of
Landscape Architecture**

Working urban watershed by urban watershed, a coalition of students, faculty, professionals and citizens envisioned what Seattle's green infrastructure network could be in the year 2100.

↓
·····························
Name: Mountains to Sound Greenway

Location: Washington State, USA

Date: 1993–

Designer: Mountains to Sound Greenway

The Mountains to Sound Greenway forms a 160-kilometre (100-mile) stretch of connected forests and farms, recreational trails and facilities, small towns and cultural features in the watersheds adjoining Interstate 90 – a major east-west freeway. Over the last 20 years, this small non-profit organization has worked to compile over 81,000 hectares (200,000 acres) of protected public lands.

Regional planning frameworks

Establishing planning frameworks at regional scales is necessary to preserve the diversity of regional cultural, physical and ecological landscapes. Regional planning approaches such as those found in New South Wales, Australia, and the Netherlands' National Ecological Network, as well as the open space plans for the New England Greenway Vision Plan and the Mountains to Sound Greenway – a 160-kilometre (100-mile) corridor aligned along a major interstate freeway in the state of Washington – are excellent examples that span a range of geographic scales and contexts.

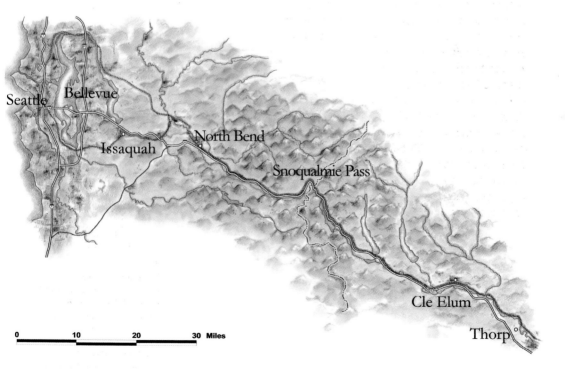

Within a ring of dense, compact cities comprising the most populated region in The Netherlands sits the Groene Hart (Green Heart), a rural agricultural and recreation area preserved for more than fifty years. The Green Heart was originally established to protect agricultural uses from encroaching residential and commercial development and to provide green space separating the growing municipalities (including Amsterdam, Utrecht, Den Haag and Rotterdam). As urban population has grown to over six million in the Randstad Region and agricultural economies have been presented with new challenges to remain viable, the recreational and biodiversity aspects of the region have become the primary values served by the Green Heart. Dominated by water bodies, the Green Heart supports a broad diversity of habitat types including peatlands, forest and agricultural lands. While the pressures of encroachment still exist and several transportation corridors now cross the preserve, a 7.2-kilometre (5-mile) tunnel for high speed rail is being constructed beneath a section of this valued open space to protect the region's character and its ecological and recreational value.

Ecological approaches:

→ Preserved green space and water bodies

→ Green space separates compact towns

→ Space for local agriculture, recreation and contact with natural systems

ㄴ←ㄴ↑

Name: Netherlands Green Heart (Groene Hart)

Location: Dutch Randstad, The Netherlands

Communities come in all sizes, from neighbourhoods, hamlets and villages to mega-metropolitan areas such as Beijing and Buenos Aires. While our societies are becoming increasingly reliant upon regional and global forces, many communities are attempting to become more self-sufficient and resilient through conservation and the local production of resources. In order to enjoy local ecological services, communities are actively working towards preserving and restoring ecological health, both within their borders and in surrounding locales that are vulnerable to degradation from development. While serving human needs in cities and towns is paramount, communities are more likely to be liveable and therefore may be more successful in curtailing sprawl when they provide ample opportunities for contact with nature.

Cities and towns

Cities are organized entities that provide services to their constituents through systems such as mobility, power, water, waste removal, health, recreation and safety. While these systems are often embedded in outmoded consumptive practices, many cities are working to become more sustainable, dedicating staff to evaluate the ecological footprints of municipal operations and the urban impacts of planning policies, codes and services, and to finding new solutions for reducing those impacts. The following pages outline some approaches that communities are taking to become more sustainable, ecological and resilient.

↑

Name: Samsø, Denmark

Location: Samsø, Denmark

The Danish island community of Samsø is energy neutral, producing enough energy through wind and biofuels to offset imports of fossil fuels.

→

Name: Times Square and Broadway

Location: New York, New York, USA

Date: 2009

Designer: Gehl Architects and Newe

New York City officials are promoting and prioritizing the integration of walking and bicycling systems into the existing urban fabric. Over a mile of Broadway and Times, Madison and Herald Squares have been transformed into pedestrian space using pavement paint, moveable furniture and planters.

Redundant circulation networks

Circulation often forms the 'bones' or physical structure of a city, both spatially and operationally. Cities with adequate density are able to support public transit, as well as shops and services that are proximate to where people reside and work. In contrast, a dispersed urban form with low density precludes the economic viability of these services, forcing a reliance upon the automobile for transport. Walking and bicycling become viable in compact communities when facilities such as trails, sidewalks, bicycle tracks and lanes, traffic calming and pedestrian-priority crossings are provided. The international popularity of City Bikes programmes such as Vélib in Paris are a testament to the public interest in active transport. Amenities such as benches and lighting also encourage walking. These redundant systems of circulation, in concert with public transit, generate resilience to petroleum shortages and support healthy conditions in cities.

Energy + Waste + Carbon

Many cities have begun to measure their carbon footprints and are looking to alternative, low-carbon forms of energy. Cities and regions in Denmark, The Netherlands and Germany are producing substantial portions of their energy from wind power; new communities in California require photovoltaics on housing; and garbage and local wood waste are burned in Denmark and Sweden to produce heat that is piped to surrounding homes and businesses. The Danish town of Samsø has become energy neutral, primarily powered by wind and biofuels. Recognizing the intense greenhouse gas impacts of methane emitted from landfills, communities such as Christchurch, New Zealand, and Seattle, USA, have begun to collect and compost food and garden waste in municipal-scale operations. The finished compost is then reused to promote plant health in parks, gardens and local agriculture.

ꜛ→
....

Name: Christchurch Composting Center

Location: Christchurch, New Zealand

Date: 2009

Owner: Living Earth Limited, under contract with the Christchurch City Council

The compost centre for the city of Christchurch collects green and kitchen waste from residents and will produce up to 65,000 tonnes of organic weed-free compost per year to improve soil quality in and around the city.

Water

Water is primarily managed in two ways in urban environments: one as supply, providing humans and other species that reside within an area with a reliable and clean source of water, and the other as waste, supporting systems that remove the wastes generated by urban areas.

Several examples of sustainable approaches to water conservation have been provided through case studies in this book. At the municipal scale, water resource planners may institute water conservation incentives and regulations, such as assistance with establishing drought-tolerant plantings, soil preparation and efficient irrigation.

Municipal systems also have the ability to transform wastewater into reuseable water for irrigation, such as at the Homebush Sydney Olympic site in Australia. Stormwater is increasingly controlled and cleansed through landscape treatment, as is currently being promoted in Seattle. There, rain gardens, rainwater harvesting and permeable alleys are being used in concert to reduce stormwater entering the sanitary system, in order to eliminate combined sewer overflows that pollute local water bodies.

In planning new development, a city's hydrological system can be wisely used as a foundation to determine the appropriate location and density of neighbourhoods so that local water resources are not degraded by new development. Christchurch's recent Southeast Area Plan demonstrates an exemplary approach.

Ecological networks + urban liveability

A city or town's 'bones' are often established through open space networks. When configured to address local landscape ecology principles these networks can provide high ecological value. Open space and ecological networks that are equitably available to all urban residents significantly increase urban liveability, providing the incentive for people to concentrate home and work in compact towns and cities.

↗→
....

Name: Sydney Olympic Park

Location: Homebush, Sydney, Australia

Date: 2000

Designer: Hargreaves Associates

In addition to landscape approaches to conserving water and protecting water resources at the former site of the 2000 Olympics, the park's water reclamation scheme includes a small-scale water treatment plant that cleans and recycles water for irrigation, fountains, and non-potable uses by residents.

CASE STUDY

Portland, Oregon, is considered one of the most progressively 'green' cities in the United States. Regulated by the state's growth management mandate and by a regional governance system, the city has established firm boundaries to contain urban development. Compact density is accompanied by an extensive multi-modal public transportation system, including interconnecting networks of light rail, streetcar, buses and an aerial tram. The city has developed an extensive system of bicycle lanes and trails – over 410 kilometres (260 miles) – that supports a popular cycling culture. Small city blocks, wide sidewalks with pedestrian amenities and urban design guidelines that promote interest at the human scale make the city's centre highly walkable.

The municipality has pioneered new approaches to detaining and treating stormwater, including almost 4.9 hectares (12 acres) of living roofs and a 'green street' programme that incorporates trees, green space and stormwater treatment in neighbourhood retrofits. Strong and artfully distinct neighbourhoods support social sustainability and liveability, incorporating historic preservation and a robust connected system of open space. This system includes the largest wilderness park in the USA (2023 hectares (5000 acres)), emphasizes stream and watershed health, and preserves connected and ecologically sensitive open space from the forested hillsides along the shores of the Willamette River. The city has established a goal of reducing greenhouse gas emissions by 80 per cent by the year 2050 through the continued expansion of mass transit, bikeways, recycling, tree planting, natural area preservation, clean energy production, education and local food production.

Ecological approaches:
→ Promotion of compact urban development
→ Multi-modal transportation options
→ Connected ecological open space system
→ Innovative stormwater treatment
→ Incentives for green buildings and energy
→ Local neighbourhood and food garden programmes

←↙↓

Name: Light Rail Transit in the Pearl District, Tanner Springs Park, Jamieson Parks and Eastbank Esplanade

Location: Portland, Oregon, USA

The term neighbourhood contains multiple interpretations, from specific districts with defined boundaries to general descriptions of areas within a larger city, town or suburb. Neighbourhoods function as localized, often social, communities that enable interaction among residents and businesses. While the formation, composition and structure of neighbourhoods vary greatly around the world and even within particular cities, they all contain the streets and sites where we live, play and work.

Landscape architects as guides

Landscape architects and urban planners often serve as designers and professional guides, assisting local jurisdictions, residents and real estate developers with integrating sustainable strategies and practices into neighbourhood development and renewal. In many countries around the world, guidelines have been developed to assist jurisdictions and neighbourhoods in planning and implementing sustainable practices. Within the United States, the US Green Building Council (USGBC) has developed a national rating system, LEED for Neighbourhoods (LEED ND) that integrates smart growth strategies into neighbourhood design. Such strategies incorporate long-term visioning and planning into neighbourhood developments that focus on creating ecologically healthy and sustainable communities.

Contextual design

As previously discussed, any approach to ecological design takes into account contextual conditions. At the neighbourhood scale, this approach builds upon the conditions that already exist while creating new value, minimizing the impacts of changes on existing and future residents. In such planning and design the environmental impacts of development on ecological conditions is also reduced, and ecologically sensitive areas are protected and preserved.

High performance | Low energy

A primary focus for ecological design is the development and implementation of high efficiency approaches to planning and design that maximize performance while reducing energy usage. The form and organization of new neighbourhood development can establish a sustainable development framework for communities. This framework often promotes the design of dense, compact neighbourhoods that integrate commercial and residential land uses, enabling social interaction and reducing energy costs associated with travel. Within individual buildings, the use of high efficiency materials and appliances, and the reuse or recycling of materials used in their construction and operations, is also prioritized.

↑

Name: GWL Terrein

Location: Amsterdam, The Netherlands

Date: 1998

Designer: West 8 Landscape Architects and Westerpark Municipal District Council

This car-free, mixed-income residential neighbourhood incorporates a generous allocation of outdoor spaces; apartments have access to roof gardens, ground-floor residents own semi-private gardens, and common open spaces are provided for local community residents.

Transportation

The energy costs associated with fossil fuel dependent forms of transportation are always high. A more sustainable approach to neighbourhood development supports mobility that promotes and incorporates transit oriented forms of development, integrating multiple forms of transportation both within and connected to nearby communities and urban centres. This approach to transportation planning incorporates pedestrian and bicycle-friendly designs and integrates high-capacity transport such as trains and light rail.

Smart growth strategies take a long-range sustainable planning approach that:

- **build on an area's unique sense of place;**
- **offer a wide a diversity of transportation alternatives, employment, and housing types;**
- **equitably distribute the costs and benefits associated with development;**
- **promote public health and preserve and enhance environmental conditions.**

Green infrastructure

As discussed in Chapter 3, the implementation of green infrastructure design and planning strategically manages the development of communities so that they conserve and enhance the ecological health, viability and services of an area. This approach takes into account the preservation or restoration of ecologically sensitive areas such as wetlands, waterways and contiguous forest patches. Yet, it also includes the integration of more engineered forms and structures, such as drainage infrastructure systems that capture, detain and treat stormwater rather than utilizing systems that simply capture and convey polluted flows to adjacent waterbodies.

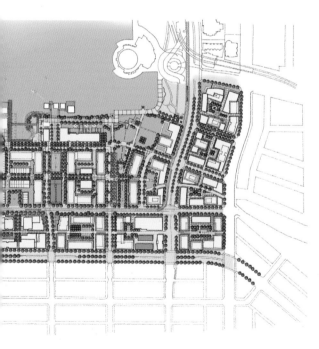

←↑

**Name: Southeast False
Creek Waterfront**

**Location: Vancouver, British
Columbia, Canada**

Date: 2005–2008

Designer: PWL Partnership

The design for the Southeast
False Creek area is Vancouver's
first comprehensive
sustainable neighbourhood
development. When fully built,
the development will house
16,000 people, incorporating
housing for a range of
incomes, recreational and
community facilities, innovative
infrastructure practices, and
access by transit and bike.

Located in Seattle, Washington, USA, the High Point neighbourhood redevelopment is internationally recognized for its innovations and achievements in the application of a sustainable and equitable approach to neighbourhood design and construction. Originally developed during the Second World War to provide government housing, the neighbourhood became a district of predominantly low-income housing through the 1990s. In 2003, the City of Seattle and community residents began working with several design firms to redevelop the housing into a mixed-income community that embraces the three primary components of equitable, quality design; a healthy environment; and an engaged community. When completed, the neighbourhood will be reconnected with the surrounding community, provide approximately 1,600 housing units with a range of options for mixed-income residents, and feature a small business district as well as neighbourhood facilities and community services.

The neighbourhood design incorporates many sustainable, smart growth strategies and practices. The overall community plan is pedestrian-friendly, reducing the need for residents to rely on automobile transportation and encouraging social interaction and physical activity. The neighbourhood plan also protected many existing trees and added more than 2,500 trees, while supplying over 8 hectares (20 acres) of parks and open space within the community. The design also incorporates an innovative natural drainage system used to manage stormwater on the site, improve water quality, and protect the habitat of a creek immediately downstream.

Ecological approaches:
→ Reuse and recycling of materials
→ Preservation of existing trees
→ Natural drainage system
→ Minimize site disturbance
→ Compact, walkable neighbourhood

↑↖←↙↓

Name: High Point Housing

Location: Seattle, Washington, USA

Date: 2000–2012

Designer: Mithun Architects; SvR Design

Streets and roadways are a fundamental infrastructure of urban areas. They enable transportation and movement within and through our communities. Yet, historically, streets in urban and residential communities also served as centres for public interactions as places of intersection between the public and private spheres of everyday life. It was along these corridors that day-to-day interactions between residents and businesses built relationships and community ties that supported neighbourhood development and character.

Street design

However, since the middle of the twentieth century, street design has been dominated by the need to accommodate the requirements and ever-growing demands of the automobile. This change commonly increased road widths to accommodate greater capacity and interspersed parking lots between businesses, reducing the feasibility, attractiveness and safety of pedestrian and bicycle travel and the use of streets as social spaces.

Landscape architects and other professionals practising urban design are developing new approaches and exploring design options for reinvigorating streetscapes that meet the requirements for automobile movement, yet are inclusive in their consideration of the multiple modes of transportation and community interaction. One aspect of this approach involves incorporating design strategies that enhance ecological conditions of streetscapes.

↑→

Name: NE Siskiyou Green Street

Location: Portland, Oregon, USA

Date: 2006

Designer: Kevin Robert Perry

This 80-year old residential street has been transformed to manage stormwater on-site using a landscape approach by disconnecting the street's runoff from the combined storm/sewer pipe system. The water is collected in a series of planted areas along the street that enable the water to be infiltrated into the soil.

Street trees

Street trees provide multiple benefits in streetscape design. Ecologically, they enhance local habitat conditions for insect and bird species, and reduce the urban heat island effect by shading roadways and sidewalks, thereby reducing the heat gain of these areas during sunny days. Functionally, they can provide both visual and physical distinctions between corridor uses by separating automobiles from bike lanes or pedestrian walkways.

Planting strips

Ecologically, planting strips provide similar functions to street trees in the creation of habitat for insect and bird species, but further enable the introduction of diversity into the streetscape. If planted with a diverse palette of species, planting strips can include flowering and fruiting species that provide valuable food sources for urban wildlife during much of the year. Planting strips can also be used to collect, detain and treat stormwater, while providing physical barriers that distinguish between multiple forms of transportation.

Stormwater infiltration + cleansing

Roadways and the impervious surfaces that surround them create run-off during rain. Polluted by petroleum products and heavy metals from the automobiles that use them, this run-off degrades the quality and ecological conditions of receiving water bodies. Ameliorating the stormwater generated by roads and surrounding impervious surfaces reduces impacts to downstream habitat. While there are many ways to design for the capture, retention and cleansing of stormwater within the right-of-way, common approaches that are integrative and improve ecological conditions include reducing the impervious area of the roadway, providing above-ground swales that capture, detain and infiltrate stormwater, and cleansing polluted water through soil infiltration and the use of plants that absorb polluting chemicals, excess nutrients and heavy metals.

Complete streets

Across the world, cities and communities are developing policies to re-establish the function of streets as an infrastructure that serves more than as automobile-centric corridors, to also facilitate other forms of transport such as walking and bicycling, and create hubs of activity that foster community identity, create healthy business environments, and provide public space for people to interact. Designing and developing streets that serve these multiple functions requires careful integration that considers safety, comfort and aesthetics for all users.

→
....
Name: Stormwater infiltration

Designer: Nevue Ngan Associates

This graphic reveals the component parts of a planting bed used for stormwater treatment and detention. The water is collected, cleansed and detained in the soil and gravel layers. Excess water not evaporated or taken up by plants is slowly conveyed through the system before being released into a receiving waterbody.

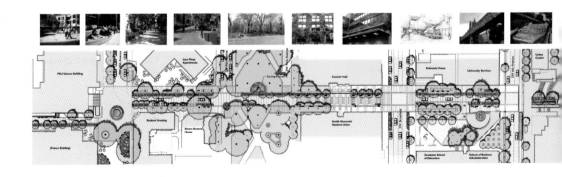

6" Thick Concrete Planter Wall
12" Depth Washed Gravel Course
48" Depth Imported Soil Mix
4" Diameter Underdrain
2" Thick Compost Mulch Layer
6" Maximum Water Retention Depth

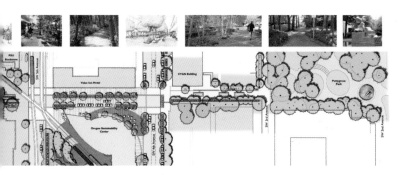

←

Name: Southwest Montgomery Complete Street

Location: Portland, Oregon, USA

Date: 2006–2011

Designer: Nevue Ngan Associates

This plan graphic illustrates the landscape architect's concept of transforming this nine-block section of Southwest Montgomery Street into a complete street. A further description is provided on the following pages.

Located in the south end of downtown Portland, bisecting the Portland State University campus, is a nine-block section of SW Montgomery Street that is currently being retrofitted as a 'complete' street. The concept for the design and plan of the street re-examines the auto-dominated public realm of the street by enhancing the pedestrian experience, providing flexible public spaces for gathering, including areas for the outdoor expansion of local businesses, increasing the number of street trees, improving wildlife habitat conditions, and implementing a sustainable approach for capturing and treating stormwater. Integrated into this vision is a multi-block plan that connects the urban fabric with themes of movement, art, plantings and water.

Once completed, the street will serve as an environmental research and stewardship opportunity for students attending the adjacent university and surrounding community. The SW Montgomery Green Street demonstrates how, in even the most urban conditions, downtown streets can be reworked to improve ecological conditions, support community character and neighbourhood engagement, maintain healthy business districts, and provide spaces for public interaction while still providing for necessary services as a transportation corridor.

Ecological approaches:
→ Preservation + planting of street trees
⇗ Enhancement of urban wildlife habitat conditions
→ Incorporation of natural drainage system
→ Provision of educational and stewardship opportunities

→↗
....
Name: SW Montgomery Street

Location: Portland, Oregon, USA

Date: 2006–2011

Designer: Nevue Ngan Associates

A robust park system and its constituent park landscapes can contribute significantly to both liveability and the ecological quality of a community. Such a system incorporates parks of varying sizes that are proximate to both residential and work places; protects the most valued landscapes in a community – such as ridgelines with views, waterfronts, creeks, wetlands and historic properties; and are connected by corridors including trails, boulevards and bikeways.

Park systems:
Ecological diversity + connectivity

A diverse, connected park system incorporates principles of landscape ecology, forming a network with patches large enough to harbour internal sensitive species, connected to smaller patches by continuous corridors to allow for wildlife movement. Ideally, these systems prioritize preservation of the most sensitive lands, such as wetlands and habitat for vulnerable species, and those that may provide the greatest biodiversity, such as stream corridors. The concepts of patch and corridor can also be applied to planning for human use of parks, with varied sizes and functions serving peoples' needs for diverse types of recreation and providing opportunities to study and experience the aesthetics of the natural environment. Connections between park patches enlarge the system for human use, enabling walking, cycling and commuting between parks.

←→
....
Name: Lurie Garden, Millennium Park

Location: Chicago, Illinois, USA

Date: 2004

Designer: Gustafson Guthrie Nichol, Piet Oudolf and Robert Israel

Part of the larger Millennium Park and linked to Chicago's 30-kilometre (18-mile) system of lakefront parks, this 2-hectare (5-acre) rooftop garden offers a rich and varied sensory experience throughout the seasons with a complex layering of more than 240 varieties of plants.

The qualities of a sustainable park:

1. It attempts to become internally self-reliant with regard to material resources. It generates materials such as soil, plants and water on-site, while reducing negative flows off-site such as fertilizer and pesticide-laden water run-off.

2. It acts as a solution to urban problems and is an antidote to urban conditions. Parks address the problems of infrastructure, reclamation, human health and social well-being.

3. It embraces temporality and change and is emblematic of ecological function and health.

Cranz and Boland, 2004

Sustainable materials + energy efficiency

Sustainable design approaches integrate practices that reduce the use of energy and material extraction in both the construction and operations phases of urban parks. These include practices such as reuse of site soils in land-shaping to reduce the costs and pollution generated in the removal or import of soils; the reuse of existing materials and structures; use of local materials from renewable resources to conserve transport energy and material sources; and consideration for the life cycle of new materials, asking the question: Can it be reused or reconstituted at the end of its current life?

Regenerative parks

Taking a regenerative approach, parklands can be used to increase ecological functioning, create new habitat areas and produce new resources. Shaping and sizing land to introduce appropriate hydrological regimes can help to catalyse and support the success of new plant and animal communities. Harvesting and reusing rainwater, greywater and wastewater generates new resources that can be used in pools, irrigation and habitat areas, such as constructed wetlands. Selection and appropriate placement of native plants, especially those that are grown from local genetic stock, can regenerate endemic ecological habitat for plants and animals. Parks may provide opportunities for generating their own energy needs, through bio-digesting waste materials, photovoltaics and passive solar heating, use of wind turbines, micro-hydro turbines installed on streams flowing over steep slopes, and the burning of tree trimmings and wood grown on the park grounds. Many urban parks now provide space and support for community gardening and urban agriculture, generating not only local food sources but also opportunities for building social connections with community neighbours.

→

Name: Westergasfabriek Culture Park

Location: Amsterdam, The Netherlands

Date: 2005

Designer: Gustafson Porter

This park represents a radical regeneration of a former gasworks industrial site. On 13 hectares (32 acres) the park offers aquatic gardens in former gasholders, market squares, an events field capable of accommodating 10,000 people, woodland areas, a stream and water gardens.

←↙

Name: Waiatarua Reserve

Location: Auckland, New Zealand

Date: 2004

Designer: City of Auckland

Formerly a drained wetland, Waiatarua Reserve was transformed into a giant stormwater treatment system that filters pollutant-carrying sediments before the city's runoff reaches Orakei Basin and Waitemata Harbour. The 20-hectare (50-acre) park is now a regenerating wetland that provides protected habitat for birds, butterflies and insects. It is also a popular place for walkers, joggers and families.

Multi-functional parks

The ecological goal of designing for diversity may also be applied to the design of parks for people. With urban space at a premium, multi-use parks that provide opportunity for diverse activities are highly valued. Urban parks that incorporate multiple activities serve diverse populations and interests, inviting regular local use and fostering a sense of safety, community and vibrancy. The incorporation of sustainable practices and opportunities for contact with other species further expands the interest and function of urban parks.

Solving bigger problems

From their inception, public parks have been conceived as agents for addressing larger issues than those found within their boundaries, by improving conditions of public health and in addressing issues of social equity. Even today, with considerable empirical research supporting both mental and physical benefits of recreational activity and physical contact with nature, the public health benefits of access to park and trail systems is used to promote their expansion and continued management. Parks and trails are also seen as urban economic and social regenerators, and are established to attract business investment in new residential and commercial areas, to uplift neighbourhoods deprived of environmental amenities and to render cities as liveable places for people of all ages. Parks and trail corridors can also be employed to ameliorate degraded conditions generated off-site, by cleaning stormwater from neighbouring streets, replacing habitat functions lost elsewhere in the locale, and sequestering carbon and cooling cities to reduce greenhouse gas pollution.

Name: Ed Benedict Skate Park

Location: Portland, Oregon, USA

Date: 2008

Designer: New Line Skateparks, with Taj Hanson

This new skate facility contributes to the park's multi-functional nature by incorporating collection and treatment of stormwater in vegetated basins that also serve as skaters' obstacles.

Park stewardship

Ongoing stewardship of park landscapes usually determines the success or failure of their sustainable and ecological performance. Staff and dedicated community members committed to enacting operations that involve conservation or regeneration of resource use are usually required. Landscape architects can greatly promote positive maintenance through the development of stewardship guides and through special training sessions that inform managers and personnel caring for ecological parks. The establishment of public partnerships and community stewardship for ongoing funding and volunteer labour are usually important, with added social benefits produced from such participatory stewardship. Often, public interest is stimulated through public participation in the design phase of a project.

←↑
....

Name: Banana Park

Location: Norrebro District, Copenhagen, Denmark

Designer: Nord Architects

This small neighbourhood park is organized in three sections that support multiple everyday uses: a 'jungle' play area; a green playing field bordered by a banana-shaped berm for sitting and sunning; and an urban plaza at the street edge with a 12-metre (40-foot) high climbing wall gateway.

Barry Curtis Park exemplifies several aspects of the sustainable and regenerative park. Located at the heart of an urban growth area near Auckland, New Zealand, the 94-hectare (232-acre) park joins with the future 20-hectare (49-acre) commercial centre of the new town of Flat Bush. Sited at the confluence of a network of waterways that drain the area, the park integrates stormwater detention and water quality treatment for the entire catchment. The design articulates natural and cultural layers to create a strong sense of place through landform, vegetation and structures, with landforms inspired by local Maori archaeological sites. Streams that were once infested with invasive exotic willow species are now growing a diverse assemblage of native plants that leave room for fluctuating storm water levels and connect back to large native forest patches upstream in the catchment.

The park features civic spaces, an 'educational axis' that provides stream access for environmental monitoring; a historic stone wall recycled and rebuilt from a nearby site; a children's play area featuring giant cut-outs of wetland birds and vegetation; and several native-themed gardens. Extensive public consultation during the design process, volunteer planting events and the diversity of activities offered in the park have been key to its early success with the community.

Ecological approaches:

→ Stream system rehabilitation

→ Detention and treatment of storm water

→ Use of permeable paving, rain gardens, gabion filtration channels and water treatment swales

→ Access to aquatic habitat for fish improved

→ Use of sustainably produced and locally sourced materials

→ Excavated materials reused in site landforms

→ Seeds sourced from nearby native plants and some plants salvaged

↓↘→
....

Name: Barry Curtis Park

Location: Flat Bush, New Zealand

Date: 2009

Designer: Isthmus

The term site is typically used to refer to the parcel of land that determines the spatial scope and boundaries of a design project. The land use of sites can include residential, commercial and industrial properties as well as schools and open space. Sites can also be privately or publicly owned. This wide variety of land use types presents opportunities for the landscape architect to pursue design strategies from a broad palette of options, while meeting the goals and objectives of a given project. Indeed, the profession of landscape architecture has established a niche market at this scale, and has developed many strategies and design techniques that capture the processes and beauty of a site through the elegant design of form and use supported by the application and integration of material and plant choices.

Site design

Over the past several decades a new aesthetic for urban site design has begun to emerge that embraces concepts directly associated with ecological design practices. This aesthetic often seeks to re-establish and re-engage the natural cycles and processes of a site. It represents a shift away from the orderly structure of trimmed lawns, manicured hedges and flower beds that has mostly dominated urban landscape design practices, to an approach that is contextually embedded, biologically diverse, productive and focused on the conservation and reuse of resources and material.

↑

Name: Southeast False Creek Waterfront

Location: Vancouver, British Columbia, Canada

Date: 2008–2009

Designer: PWL Partnership

The reuse of materials found on or near a particular site often creates a diverse palette of opportunity, but further reduces costs associated with the production and transportation of new materials to the site.

→

Name: Dockside Green

Location: Victoria, British Columbia, Canada

Date: 2009 (Phase 1)

Designer: Busby Perkins + Will (Architects) and PWL Partnership, Landscape Architects

This 6-hectare (15-acre) residential project located on Victoria's Inner Harbour is built on a former brownfield site. The design utilizes innovative technologies such as a biomass gasification plant, solar power technologies and on-site sewage treatment to clean water for non-potable reuse.

Native plants + planting design

Plants that are endemic or native to a particular landscape have adapted to the climatic conditions of that region; once established, few resources are required to maintain them. Their use in a landscape design also provides habitat for wildlife species. Developing planting designs that establish and support a multi-layered habitat of canopy trees, small trees, woody and perennial shrubs, native grasses and ground covers further increases the biodiversity of a site and can support a broader range of species. While the use of specifically native plantings is recommended, some projects may require the use of plants that are not endemic to the region. In such instances, non-invasive species that are appropriate for the site conditions should be utilized.

Material reuse + recycling

The reuse and recycling of existing materials on a site has obvious benefits in the reduction of energy required to produce and transport new materials to a site. The options here for site design are numerous, including using recycled concrete as material for retaining walls or reusing old lumber on-site to create planters. Another efficient means of reuse is the on-site composting of organic material and debris, including kitchen waste, to produce nutrient-rich soils that can be used to supplement existing soils. Compost also serves as mulch that conserves water by capturing and retaining moisture while also reducing evaporation rates from the soil.

Water harvesting

Rainwater harvesting includes both active and passive approaches to the collection and use of rainwater on-site. Passive approaches include the preparation of organic soils that collect rainwater and reduce run-off from a site. One approach to passive harvesting is the creation of rain gardens that collect precipitation and run-off in a planting bed. These gardens retain and infiltrate rainwater during wet periods, but dry out after the rains have ended. More active approaches include the actual capture and retention of run-off generated by impervious surfaces such as roofs, sidewalks and driveways in tanks or barrels. This stored water is then used to supplement water supply during drier periods.

Structural adaptation + green technologies

Another example of an ecological approach to landscape design is in the adaptation of structures to support plant growth. A common example of this type of adaptive design is the construction of vegetated or green roofs and walls. This strategy is becoming increasingly common on a wide range of land uses and structure types such as public buildings, commercial properties and residences. These structures serve to harvest and use rainwater to support plant growth, create and support habitat for bird and insect species, and if applied across a large enough expanse, it is believed that they may assist in reducing the urban heat island effect.

Maintenance

The maintenance of designed landscapes can be time consuming and is often associated with high energy costs. Applying ecologically based landscape design strategies can reduce the time and costs associated with maintenance.

→
....
Name: UNESCO Rooftop Wetland

Location: Seoul, Republic of Korea

Designer: UNESCO

Constructed as an intensive rooftop garden, this project incorporates a lined wetland that supports the growth of a wide range of aquatic and terrestrial plant species.

↑→

Name: The Orchard House

Location: Seattle, Washington, USA

Designer: Five Dot Design Build

The design of this residential parcel preserves portions of a historic orchard, utilizes recycled materials for construction, collects and detains stormwater runoff on site, and uses a palette of native plants.

CASE STUDY

Municipalities are implementing new types of land use codes and standards to promote ecological function in public and private landscapes. In its bid to become the 'City of Tomorrow,' the City of Malmö, Sweden, implemented its Quality Programme for the Western Harbour District. The programme establishes sustainable water, energy, transport, and ecological and open space standards for the development of public infrastructure, and for the design and construction of privately developed buildings and neighbourhoods.

The City of Berlin has implemented a similar programme named the BioType Area Factor (BAF). Berlin's programme focuses on improving the liveability and ecological conditions of the urban core, using a formulaic approach to establish goals and measure the capacity of site design to promote high-quality, ecological urban development.

Building on these established programmes, in 2007 the City of Seattle, Washington, USA, began implementing the Seattle Green Factor. The first of its kind in the country, the programme enables greater regulatory latitude for open space while increasing the ecological function and aesthetic qualities of privately developed urban sites. Basing its requirements on the employment of functional systems rather than adherence to rigid spatial standards, the programme promotes site designs that establish a higher level of biological diversity, integrate building architecture with desired landscape processes and improve the ecological conditions of the city through features such as living roofs, green walls, permeable paving and large tree retention.

Ecological approaches:
→ Promotes the use of ecological design strategies

→ Provides educational and design standards

→ Highlights the potential of integrating ecological design practices into urban environments

A – Modular trellis
B – Raised bed planters
C – Planting area
D – Overhead structure
E – 2" green roof
F – Roof deck
G – Planting area
H – 4" green roof
I – Overhanging plants
J – Vines on cable system
K – Stormwater planter
L – Overhead structure
M – Water feature
N – Rain garden
O – Cistern
P – Entry court
Q – Sidewalk
R – Planting strip with street
S – Street

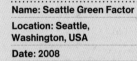

Name: Seattle Green Factor

Location: Seattle, Washington, USA

Date: 2008

Designer: City of Seattle, Graphics by The Berger Partnership

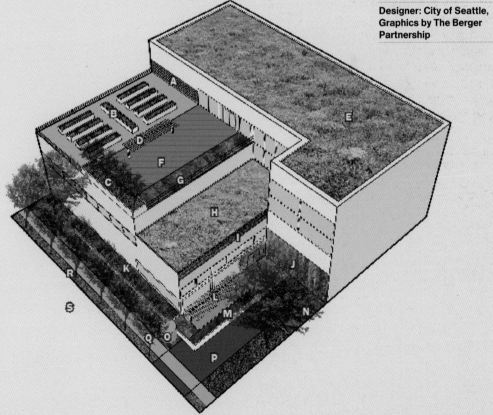

Ecological design represents the integration of living and built worlds. By focusing on the natural processes that both form and maintain life as we know it, landscape architects can more adeptly serve to enhance ecological conditions for humans and all forms of life. This is no easy undertaking; adapting our modes and methods of design to a more ecologically sound approach is an uphill battle. Yet, in many countries, regions, cities, neighbourhoods and homes around the world, a new ethic is emerging that embraces ecological planning, design and management.

Landscape architects can play a critical role in bridging the conceptual divide that often separates the perception of the natural world from human environments. As designers and stewards of our built environments, landscape architects have the opportunity to translate the processes and functions that maintain our environments into designs that repair, regenerate and enhance conditions affecting the ecological health of our urban communities.

This book has introduced you to the potential that ecological design has to inform the allied design and planning professions. It provides a framework for continuing the discourse and exploring the connections between landscape architecture and its role in designing, constructing and maintaining our built environments in ways that will link human and environmental health for future generations.

←
....
Name: Travis Wetland
Nature Heritage Park
....
Location: Christchurch,
New Zealand
....
Date: 1993
....
Designer: Colin Meurk and
Friends of Travis Wetland
....
Visionary planners and
dedicated volunteers have
transformed a former derelict
pasture and swamp into a
116-hectare (287-acre) high-
functioning wetland that serves
as an important component in
the city's open space network.

Chapter 1

1. What design or planning projects do you know that are helping to make cities more ecologically sustainable and healthy?

2. What experiences have you had in cities where you have felt the benefits – restorative, recreational, educational, health or otherwise – of contact with the natural world? What design actions might have created those opportunities?

3. What could be done in your city to improve its ecological conditions and functioning?

Chapter 2

1. Define the component parts of a natural system with which you are familiar. Draw a diagram of the relationships between these parts and determine the overall function of the system.

2. Next, draw a diagram of the components and relationships of a built system that you are familiar with.

3. Look for and identify the potential for overlap between these systems. How would you, as a designer, manipulate this connection in systems to improve ecosystem health, and the condition and/ or operations of both systems involved? For example, how might the implementation of green infrastructure lead to increased biodiversity?

Chapter 3

Select a block within your neighbourhood and map internal patches, edges and connective corridors. (Do not necessarily choose a park or open space, but think about how concepts in landscape ecology can be translated to other forms and urban conditions.)

1. How does this block fit within the matrix of the larger landscape conditions?

2. What processes are important to consider when developing an understanding of this block? Which are important for maintaining the character and function of the place? What do you think is missing?

3. As a designer, how would you harness these processes to increase resiliency in the natural and built systems within the block and surrounding neighbourhood? How might designs for the block or sites within it catalyse processes that regenerate resources or foster local biodiversity?

Chapter 4

Sketch the conditions of a hypothetical site of established ecological integrity that includes a stream and wetland, bisected by a road, with residential and commercial development located to one side.

1. Based on this situation, determine where and why you would site a new housing development and associated infrastructure. How might you avoid or mitigate impacts to the stream and wetland? How might you avoid producing off-site impacts, or, even better, accept and mitigate impacts from the adjacent development?

2. How might you engage community members in a participatory design project? What techniques and tools might you use to actively elicit sincere, informed and creative community responses?

3. How can a landscape architect help to ensure the successful construction and long-term stewardship of a project? Name at least six strategies.

Chapter 5

1. In the hypothetical site you sketched in Chapter 4, which of the operations described in this chapter might help it to achieve greater ecological integrity or resiliency? Draw a diagram of how these operations might be applied to your site.

2. Develop your own operational metaphor for describing a landscape process and associated form that could engender ecological health. Describe the operation and give it a title.

3. Relate and apply your metaphorical operation to some aspect or condition of a project that you know, or any of the case studies provided in the book.

Chapter 6

Select a green space in your neighbourhood or community.

1. Draw a diagram of the hierarchy of nested spatial scales of which your site is a part, for example a neighbourhood, community, watershed, region.

2. Map the other green spaces that could be connected to your site. Where could stronger linkages be made to extend and create a more robust open space network? What would you prioritize?

3. What are the opportunities for your site to improve the ecological integrity of your neighbourhood, community or watershed? List the strategies you would employ, based upon the concepts presented in this book.

Bibliography

Ahern, Jack; Leduc, Elisabeth and York, Mary Lee. **Biodiversity Planning and Design, Sustainable Practices**. Island Press, Washington, DC, 2006.

Beatley, Timothy. **Green Urbanism, Learning from European Cities**. Island Press, Washington, DC, 2000.

Bekkers, Gaston. **Designed Dutch Landscape: Jac. P. Thijsse Park**. Architectura and Natura with the Garden Art Press, Amsterdam, 2003.

Burns, Carol and Kahn, Andrea Eds. **Site Matters**. Routledge, New York and London, 2005.

Cranz, Galen, and Boland, Michael 'Defining the Sustainable Park: A Fifth Model for Urban Parks,' **Landscape Journal** 23:2-04. 2004.

Dramstad, Wenche; Olson, James and Forman, Richard. **Landscape Ecology Principles in Landscape Architecture and Land-Use Planning**. Island Press, Washington DC, 1996.

Dreiseitl, Herbert and Grau, Dieter. **New Waterscapes: Planning, Building and Designing with Water**. Birkhäuser, Basel, Boston, 2005.

Farr, Douglas. **Sustainable Urbanism: Urban Design with Nature**. John Wiley and Sons, Inc., New York, 2008.

France, Robert. **Handbook of Regenerative Landscape Design**. CRC Press, Boca Raton and London, 2008.

Gehl, Jan. **Cities for People**. Island Press, Washington DC, 2010.

Hough, Michael. **Cities and Natural Process**. Routledge, London and New York, 1995.

Johnson, Bart and Hill, Kristina. **Ecology and Design: Frameworks for Learning**. Island Press, Washington, DC, 2002.

Kellert, Stephen R and Wilson, Edward O. **The Biophilia Hypothesis**. Island Press, Washington DC, 1993.

Lyle, John Tillman. **Regenerative Design for Sustainable Development**. John Wiley and Sons, Inc, New York, 1994.

McDonough, William and Braungart, Michael. **Cradle to Cradle: Remaking the Way We Make Things**. North Point Press, New York, 2002.

McHarg, Ian. **Design with Nature**. John Wiley and Sons, Inc., New York, 1992 (original publication, the Natural History Press, 1969).

Meadows, Donella. **Thinking in Systems: A Primer.** Chelsea Green Publishing: White River Junction, Vermont, 2008.

Melby, Pete and Cathcart, Tom. **Regenerative Design Techniques**. John Wiley and Sons, Inc., New York, 2002.

Mostafavi, Mohsen. **Ecological Urbansim**. Lars Muller, Baden, 2010.

Newman, Peter; Beatley, Timothy and Boyer, Heather. **Resilient Cities: Responding to Peak Oil and Climate Change**. Island Press, Washington DC, 2009.

Ndubisi, Forster. **Ecological Planning: A Historical and Comparative Synthesis**. Johns Hopkins University Press, Baltimore and London, 2002.

Perlman, Dan L and Midler, Jeffrey C. **Practical Ecology for Planners, Developers, and Citizens**. Island Press, Washington DC, 2005.

Potteiger, Matthew and Purinton, Jamie. **Landscape Narratives: Design Practices for Telling Stories**. John Wiley and Sons, Inc, New York, 1998.

Schaefer, Valentin, Rudd, Hillary and Vala, Jamie. **Urban Biodiversity: Exploring Natural Habitat and its Value in Cities**. Captus Press, Ontario, 2004.

Spirn, Anne Whiston. **The Granite Garden: Urban Nature and Human Design**. Basic Books, New York, 1984.

Steiner, Frederick. **The Living Landscape: An Ecological Approach to Landscape Planning**, 2nd Ed. Island Press, Washington DC, 2008.

Stitt, Fred A. Ed. **Ecological Design Handbook**. McGraw-Hill, New York, 1999.

Thompson, George F and Steiner, Fredrick R. **Ecological Design and Planning**. John Wiley & Sons, New York, 1997.

Thompson, J. William and Sorvig, Kim. **Sustainable Landscape Construction: A Guide to Green Building Outdoors**. Island Press, Washington, DC 2000.

Van der Ryn, Sim and Cowan, Stuart. **Ecologicial Design**, 2nd Ed. Island Press, Washington DC, 2007.

Waldheim, Charles. **The Landscape Urbanism Reader**, Princeton Architectural Press, New York, 2006.

Walker, Brian and Salt, David. **Resilience Thinking: Sustaining Ecosystems and People in a Changing World**, Island Press, Washington DC, 2006.

Web resources

American Society of Landscape Architects
www.asla.org

CABE - Commission for Architecture and the Built Environment
www.cabe.org.uk/

Ecological Society of America
www.esa.org/

Green Futures Lab
www.greenfutures.washington.edu

International Federation of Landscape Architects (IFLA)
www.iflaonline.org

International Living Building Institute
www.ilbi.org/

i-Sustain
www.i-sustain.com

Landscape Architecture Foundation, Landscape Performance Series
**www.lafoundation.org/research/
landscape-performance-series/**

Landscape Architecture Resource
**www.landscapearchitecture
resource.com**

Landscape Institute
www.landscapeinstitute.org/

Landscape + Urbanism
www.landscapeandurbanism.blogspot.com

Land8Lounge
www.land8lounge.com

Regenerative Design Institute
www.regenerativedesign.org

The Society for Ecological Restoration
www.ser.org

Sustainable Cities
www.sustainablecities.dk

Sustainable Sites Initiative
www.sustainablesites.org/

Urban Ecology
www.urbanecology.org

Urban Land Institute
www.uli.org

World Landscape Architect
www.worldlandscapearchitect.com

World Resources Institute
www.wri.org

Professional journals

Ecological Management & Restoration
**http://www.wiley.com/bw/journal.
asp?ref=1442-7001**

Ecology and Society
www.ecologyandsociety.org

Garten + Landschaft (Germany)
www.garten-landschaft.de

Green Places
www.landscape.co.uk/greenplaces/journal

IFLA Online Journal
www.iflajournal.org

The International Journal of Environmental, Cultural, Economic and Social Sustainability
http://onsustainability.com/journal/

Journal of Chinese Landscape Architecture
**http://en.cnki.com.cn/Journal_
en/C-C038-ZGYL-2001-06.htm**

Journal of Green Building
www.collegepublishing.us/journal.htm

Journal of Landscape Architecture
www.info-jola.de/

Landscape Architecture Australia
www.aila.org.au/landscapeaustralia

Landscape Architecture New Zealand
www.agm.co.nz

Landscape Journal
http://lj.uwpress.org/

Landscape Paysages (Canada)
www.csla.ca

Landscape and Urban Planning
**http://www.sciencedirect.com/science/
journal/01692046**

Landskab (Denmark)
www.arkfo.dk

Places Journal
www.places-journal.org

Terrain.org: A Journal of Built and Natural Environments
www.terrain.org

Topos: The International Review of Landscape Architecture and Urban Design
www.topos.de

Urban Habitats
www.urbanhabitats.org/

Index

Ecological Design

Compiled by Indexing Specialists (UK) Ltd

Acknowledgements and picture credits

Acknowledgements

We would like to express our sincere gratitude to the design firms and individuals who generously supplied images and provided information about the projects featured in this book. We are also deeply appreciative of our home institution, the Department of Landscape Architecture and College of Built Environments at the University of Washington, Seattle. The agenda and interdisciplinary focus of this institution enables faculty and students to explore theories and applications across a broad scope of interests in the built environment, and particularly urban ecological design. Specifically, we would like to thank Tera Hatfield for her research and development of diagrammatic images.

At AVA Publishing we are grateful to Renée Last for her patience, openness to presentation approaches, and artful editing. Lynsey Brough assisted with sourcing many of the book images, and Atelier David Smith (www.atelier.ie) designed the book.

We are especially indebted to our families, particularly our partners Paul and Anna, who patiently supported us as we developed the book's narrative, visited projects, and immersed ourselves in understanding and furthering the principles and practices of ecological design.

Publisher's note

The subject of ethics is not new, yet its consideration within the applied visual arts is perhaps not as prevalent as it might be. Our aim here is to help a new generation of students, educators and practitioners find a methodology for structuring their thoughts and reflections in this vital area.

AVA Publishing hopes that these **Working with ethics** pages provide a platform for consideration and a flexible method for incorporating ethical concerns in the work of educators, students and professionals. Our approach consists of four parts:

The **introduction** is intended to be an accessible snapshot of the ethical landscape, both in terms of historical development and current dominant themes.

The **framework** positions ethical consideration into four areas and poses questions about the practical implications that might occur. Marking your response to each of these questions on the scale shown will allow your reactions to be further explored by comparison.

The **case study** sets out a real project and then poses some ethical questions for further consideration. This is a focus point for a debate rather than a critical analysis so there are no predetermined right or wrong answers.

A selection of **further reading** for you to consider areas of particular interest in more detail.

Ethical: aware-ness/ reflect-ion/ debate

Introduction

Ethics is a complex subject that interlaces the idea of responsibilities to society with a wide range of considerations relevant to the character and happiness of the individual. It concerns virtues of compassion, loyalty and strength, but also of confidence, imagination, humour and optimism. As introduced in ancient Greek philosophy, the fundamental ethical question is: *what should I do?* How we might pursue a 'good' life not only raises moral concerns about the effects of our actions on others, but also personal concerns about our own integrity.

In modern times the most important and controversial questions in ethics have been the moral ones. With growing populations and improvements in mobility and communications, it is not surprising that considerations about how to structure our lives together on the planet should come to the forefront. For visual artists and communicators, it should be no surprise that these considerations will enter into the creative process.

Some ethical considerations are already enshrined in government laws and regulations or in professional codes of conduct. For example, plagiarism and breaches of confidentiality can be punishable offences. Legislation in various nations makes it unlawful to exclude people with disabilities from accessing information or spaces. The trade of ivory as a material has been banned in many countries. In these cases, a clear line has been drawn under what is unacceptable.

But most ethical matters remain open to debate, among experts and lay-people alike, and in the end we have to make our own choices on the basis of our own guiding principles or values. Is it more ethical to work for a charity than for a commercial company? Is it unethical to create something that others find ugly or offensive?

Specific questions such as these may lead to other questions that are more abstract. For example, is it only effects on humans (and what they care about) that are important, or might effects on the natural world require attention too?

Is promoting ethical consequences justified even when it requires ethical sacrifices along the way? Must there be a single unifying theory of ethics (such as the Utilitarian thesis that the right course of action is always the one that leads to the greatest happiness of the greatest number), or might there always be many different ethical values that pull a person in various directions?

As we enter into ethical debate and engage with these dilemmas on a personal and professional level, we may change our views or change our view of others. The real test though is whether, as we reflect on these matters, we change the way we act as well as the way we think. Socrates, the 'father' of philosophy, proposed that people will naturally do 'good' if they know what is right. But this point might only lead us to yet another question: *how do we know what is right?*

You

What are your ethical beliefs?

Central to everything you do will be your attitude to people and issues around you. For some people, their ethics are an active part of the decisions they make every day as a consumer, a voter or a working professional. Others may think about ethics very little and yet this does not automatically make them unethical. Personal beliefs, lifestyle, politics, nationality, religion, gender, class or education can all influence your ethical viewpoint.

Using the scale, where would you place yourself? What do you take into account to make your decision? Compare results with your friends or colleagues.

Your client

What are your terms?

Working relationships are central to whether ethics can be embedded into a project, and your conduct on a day-to-day basis is a demonstration of your professional ethics. The decision with the biggest impact is whom you choose to work with in the first place. Cigarette companies or arms traders are often-cited examples when talking about where a line might be drawn, but rarely are real situations so extreme. At what point might you turn down a project on ethical grounds and how much does the reality of having to earn a living affect your ability to choose?

Using the scale, where would you place a project? How does this compare to your personal ethical level?

01 02 03 04 05 06 07 08 09 10

01 02 03 04 05 06 07 08 09 10

Your specifications

What are the impacts of your materials?

In relatively recent times, we are learning that many natural materials are in short supply. At the same time, we are increasingly aware that some man-made materials can have harmful, long-term effects on people or the planet. How much do you know about the materials that you use? Do you know where they come from, how far they travel and under what conditions they are obtained? When your creation is no longer needed, will it be easy and safe to recycle? Will it disappear without a trace? Are these considerations your responsibility or are they out of your hands?

Using the scale, mark how ethical your material choices are.

Your creation

What is the purpose of your work?

Between you, your colleagues and an agreed brief, what will your creation achieve? What purpose will it have in society and will it make a positive contribution? Should your work result in more than commercial success or industry awards? Might your creation help save lives, educate, protect or inspire? Form and function are two established aspects of judging a creation, but there is little consensus on the obligations of visual artists and communicators toward society, or the role they might have in solving social or environmental problems. If you want recognition for being the creator, how responsible are you for what you create and where might that responsibility end?

Using the scale, mark how ethical the purpose of your work is.

01 02 03 04 05 06 07 08 09 10

01 02 03 04 05 06 07 08 09 10

Working with ethics

Working with publicly owned spaces is an aspect of landscape architecture that involves the discipline with issues of politics, society and ethics. The creation or restoration of public parks and buildings, housing estates, city squares, infrastructure or coastlines is a multidisciplinary activity where decisions can have large-scale consequences. Projects often reflect social attitudes of the time towards nature, communities, integration and freedom of movement. The best interests of the public should ideally be maintained, but this might be difficult amongst conflicting pressures from financial interests or political reputations. Similarly, what might benefit the taxpayer may have an adverse impact on the natural environment. Having a clear ethical stance or code of conduct from the outset can be crucial to negotiating such conflicts with any conviction. Consulting with the public or directly involving them with the design process is one possible route to pursuing a more inclusive, diverse and ethical approach to creating public spaces. At the same time this might adversely create feelings of animosity or it could be considered an act of tokenism that only incurs the need for more time and money.

Landscape architect Andrew Jackson Downing first voiced and publicized the need for New York's Central Park in 1844. Supporters were primarily the wealthy, who admired the public grounds of London and Paris, and argued that New York needed a similar facility to establish its international reputation. The state appointed a Central Park Commission to oversee the development and in 1857, a landscape design contest was held. Writer Frederick Law Olmsted and English architect Calvert Vaux developed the Greensward Plan, which was selected as the winning design.

Before construction could start, the designated area had to be cleared of its inhabitants, most of whom were poor and either African Americans or immigrants. Roughly 1,600 people were evicted under the rule of 'eminent domain', which allowed the government to seize private property for public purposes.

Following its completion in 1873, the park quickly slipped into decline. This was largely due to lack of interest from the New York authorities. Times were also changing – cars had been invented and were becoming commonplace. No longer were parks used only for walks and picnics, people now wanted space for sports.

In 1934, Fiorello LaGuardia was elected mayor of New York City and gave Robert Moses the job of cleaning up Central Park. Lawns and trees were replanted, walls were sandblasted, bridges were repaired and major redesigning and construction work was carried out (19 playgrounds and 12 ball fields were created). By the 1970s, Central Park had become a venue for public events on an unprecedented scale, including political rallies and demonstrations, festivals and massive concerts. But at the same time, the city of New York was in economic and social crisis. Morale was low and crime was high. Central Park saw an era of vandalism, territorial use and illicit activity. As a result, several citizen groups emerged to reclaim the park and called for proper planning and management.

The outcome was the establishment of the office of Central Park Administrator and the founding of the Central Park Conservancy. Central Park was redesigned with a revolutionary zone-management system. Every zone has a specific individual accountable for its day-to-day maintenance. As of 2007, the Conservancy had invested approximately USD$450 million in restoration and management. Today, Central Park is the most visited park in the United States with around 25 million visitors annually.

What responsibility does a landscape architect have to ensure a public space is maintained once it is complete?

Was it unethical to evict people in order to build a public park? Would this happen today?

Would you have worked on this project?

Commissioned by clients to install barrier walls and private pathways that can keep out or discourage those who are unwanted, or hired to create private commercial experiences out of what may have been public space, many become complicit in structuring the urban language of separation.

Ellen Posner
(former architecture critic)

Working with ethics

AIGA
Design Business and Ethics
2007, AIGA

Eaton, Marcia Muelder
Aesthetics and the Good Life
1989, Associated University Press

Ellison, David
Ethics and Aesthetics in European Modernist Literature:
From the Sublime to the Uncanny
2001, Cambridge University Press

Fenner, David E W (Ed)
Ethics and the Arts:
An Anthology
1995, Garland Reference Library of Social Science

Gini, Al and Marcoux, Alexei M
Case Studies in Business Ethics
2005, Prentice Hall

McDonough, William and Braungart, Michael
Cradle to Cradle:
Remaking the Way We Make Things
2002, North Point Press

Papanek, Victor
Design for the Real World:
Making to Measure
1972, Thames & Hudson

United Nations Global Compact
The Ten Principles
www.unglobalcompact.org/AboutTheGC/TheTenPrinciples/index.html